PRAISE FOR GLOBAL TEAMS

"Marquardt and Horvath have developed a provocative global teaming model that can be applied to all industries in the world of emerging e-markets. Their work transcends a tactical approach for organizations and blends theory and practice through the use of real case study research."
    Mary Kay Vona, Partner, PricewaterhouseCoopers

"*Global Teams* provides practical guidelines and real-world examples that address critical issues so often overlooked by senior executives making policies and developing strategies. The authors make a significant contribution to improving business effectiveness in the 21st century."
    Les Pickett, President, Asian Regional Training and Development Organisation;
    Past International President, Institute of Business Administration

"Few phenomena are affecting today's commerce as powerfully as the globalization of industry. Few challenges are more central to this process and to the success of these efforts than the building of teams relevant and effective in global action environments. This book gives strong focus to that challenge and its resolution."
    Robert Morris, Ph.D., Director, Management Training
    and Development Institute

"A superb book demonstrating how to use technology to connect with speeding information, how to achieve more powerfully than a single person could, and how to leap complex global problems in a single bound. If you want to know how to accelerate corporate global success, *Global Teams* has it all."
    Francesco Sofo, Team Leader for Projects Development USA
    & Canada, University of Canberra (Australia)

"This book indicates to global team leaders ways and means of meeting the challenges. It is a very helpful book to those whose team thoughts and communications have to be at the speed of light."
    Dr. Charles Margerison, CEO, Trainingalliances.com and Myjob.com

"The timing could not be better for this well-researched book. *Global Teams* prepares executives, managers, and professionals worldwide for the future of work, organization, and life. It is a book for everyone doing business in the era of globalization."
    Mohd Effendy Rajab, Vice Chairman, Adult Resources,
    Asia Pacific Region, and National Training Commissioner,
    Singapore Scout Association

"Marquardt and Horvath have distilled their years of hands-on experience into a practical guide to working globally with diverse teams. If you are dealing with cross-cultural issues, global expansion, distributed work, and the need to meet tight schedules, this book will help. Buy it today!"
> Kevin B. Wheeler, President and Founder, Global Learning Resources, Inc.

"This book covers various critical issues concerning global teams building. In the information society, global teams can take maximum advantage of the powerful capabilities of advanced information technologies. Marquardt and Horvath have done an excellent job of discussing how technology can support global teams."
> Dr. Badrul H. Khan, Associate Professor, Educational Technology Leadership, George Washington University

GLOBAL TEAMS

GLOBAL TEAMS

HOW TOP MULTINATIONALS SPAN BOUNDARIES AND CULTURES WITH HIGH-SPEED TEAMWORK

MICHAEL J. MARQUARDT
LISA HORVATH

DAVIES-BLACK PUBLISHING
Palo Alto, California

First reprinted by Davies-Black, an imprint of Nicholas Brealey Publishing, in 2012

A Nicholas Brealey Publishing Company
20 Park Plaza, Suite 610
Boston, MA 02116 USA
Tel: 617-523-3801
Fax: 617-523-3708

Nicholas Brealey Publishing
3-5 Spafield Street, Clerkenwell
London, EC1R 4QB, UK

Tel: +44-(0)-207-239-0360
Fax: +44-(0)-207-239-0370

www.nicholasbrealey.com

Published by Davies-Black Publishing, an imprint of Consulting Psychologists Press, Inc., 3803 East Bayshore Road, Palo Alto, CA 94303; 800-624-1765.

Special discounts on bulk quantities of Davies-Black books are available to corporations, professional associations, and other organizations. For details, contact the Director of Book Sales at Davies-Black Publishing, an imprint of Consulting Psychologists Press, Inc., 3803 East Bayshore Road, Palo Alto, CA 94303; 650-691-9123; fax 650-623-9271.

Copyright © 2001 by Davies-Black Publishing, an imprint of Consulting Psychologists Press, Inc. All rights reserved. No part of this book may be reproduced, stored in a retrieval system, or transmitted in any form or by any means, electronic, mechanical, photocopying, recording, or otherwise, without written permission of the publisher, except in the case of brief quotations embodied in critical articles or reviews.

Davies-Black and colophon are registered trademarks of Consulting Psychologists Press, Inc.

Visit the Davies-Black Publishing web site at www.daviesblack.com.

16 15 14 13   3 4 5 6 7 8 9 10
Printed in the United States of America

Library of Congress Cataloging-in-Publication Data
Marquardt, Michael J.
  Global teams : how top multinationals span boundaries and cultures with high-speed teamwork/ Michael J. Marquardt, Lisa Horvath.
      p. cm.
  Includes bibliographical references and index.
  ISBN 9780891064046
  1. International business enterprises—Management. 2. Intercultural communication. 3. Teams in the workplace. I. Horvath, Lisa II. Title.

HD62.4 .M3679 2001
658.4'036—dc21
                                                                    2001028573

FIRST EDITION
First printing 2001

Contents

Preface ix
About the Authors xiii

Part One

THE CORNERSTONES 1

1. The Power of Global Teams 3
2. Five Challenges Facing Global Teams 19

Part Two

BRIDGES AND BOUNDARIES 41

3. Effective Leadership 43
4. Creating a Vision and Team Identity 67
5. Building Swift Trust and Strong Norms 81

Part Three

CULTURAL AND TECHNOLOGICAL FOUNDATIONS 99

6. Capturing the Power of Cultural Diversity 101
7. Technological Support and Communications 119

Part Four

ALIGNING THE HUMAN RESOURCES 141

  8 Harnessing Cultural, Interpersonal, and Technical Expertise 143
  9 Global Team Facilitators 157
10 Measurement and Feedback Systems 179
11 Team-Oriented Assessment and Rewards 193
12 Building Global Teams for the Twenty-first Century 203

Appendix A: GlobalTeams Capability and Readiness Profile 223
Appendix B: Web Sites on Global Teams 229
References 233
Index 239

Preface

The building of global teams has quickly become *the* business challenge of the twenty-first century. More and more companies now recognize that succeeding in the global marketplace cannot occur without strong and effective global teams. The powerful, creative dynamics of global teamwork is, according to Devereaux and Johansen (1994), "the electricity that lights up the global economy." Every day, thousands of companies around the world will need to call upon their people to work in global teams, to communicate and cooperate across radically different cultures, to manage widely dispersed, fragmented organizations, and to hurdle multiple time zones in a single bound.

Although a rapidly growing number of companies now use global teams, most organizational efforts are failures—failures caused by barriers of distances and time zones, by language and cultural differences, by communications texts and contexts, by too little or too much communications. These challenges have become so great that the essence of teamness is never created and the efforts of the fledgling teams are lost in the darkness of global space and cyberspace.

How then can we create teams that will work well across the barriers of diversity and distance? How do we build teams that are united by a common vision and purpose but encourage diversity of thinking and actions? What sort of leaders are best for teams that may never meet and who work around the clock and around the globe? How do you build trust, motivate members, schedule meetings, and get things done well and on time while working with people of numerous functional, corporate, and national cultures, many of which clash with one another?

GLOBAL TEAMS

WHY THIS BOOK?

To answer these questions is the challenge of this book. Based on extensive research and experience with global teams in every part of the world, we have developed an array of steps and strategies to show readers how to become effective leaders and members of global teams. The book presents the theoretical foundations as well as the practical principles that are needed for developing and implementing the work of global teams. The GlobalTeams Model, which is discussed and applied throughout the book, provides a clear framework for organizations to build effective global teams—teams that can quickly and successfully form and function and produce.

OVERVIEW OF THE BOOK

Part I presents an overview of the pull and resistance of global teams: how teams can generate the power to accelerate corporate success but also the powerful difficulties that can lead to corporate failure. In Chapter 1, the ten benefits that accrue to global teams are presented together with examples of how teams achieved these successes. Chapter 2 discusses the five major challenges of global teams: cultural diversity, geographic distance, coordination and control, communications, and teamness.

The next three parts of the book present the GlobalTeams Model: bridges and boundaries (Part II), foundations (Part III), and human resource alignments (Part IV). In Part II we look at the bridges and boundaries. Chapter 3 examines the roles, skills, and attributes of effective leaders of global teams. Chapter 4 investigates how a team can create the challenging vision and shared identity critical for global teams. Chapter 5 considers the importance of building trust and strong group norms before tackling the tasks facing the global team.

Part III presents the two foundation stones for global teams: culture and technology. Chapter 6 explores the richness created by cultural diversity and shows how this diversity can be converted into powerful synergies of innovative thinking and action. In Chapter 7 we show how the various informational and learning technologies can be tapped to maximize their support of global teams.

PREFACE

Part IV concludes the GlobalTeams Model by presenting the aligning factors necessary to support the work of global teams. Chapter 8 examines the strategies for the selection, development, and retention of global team members. Chapter 9 looks at the role of a global team facilitator—someone who focuses on assuring that the dynamic process of the team continues despite an array of time pressures, group challenges, and global distances. Although few global teams use a facilitator, the role is increasingly seen as critical for the survival and success of global teams. Chapter 10 describes the measurement and feedback systems for global teams, and in Chapter 11 we explore the important component of team assessments and rewards. Chapter 12, the final chapter, presents a twelve-step guide with specific strategies on how organizations can initiate, develop, build, and optimize global teams. This chapter also explains how the benefits of global teams can be transferred throughout the organization.

Case studies illustrating the workings, difficulties, and successes of global teams are interwoven throughout all the chapters. These cases come from all parts of the world. Many are written by global team members themselves. In addition, readers will discover a number of worksheets and diagrams to assist in applying the book's contents to their own situation. Appendix A contains the GlobalTeams Profile to measure and assess the status of global teams; Appendix B presents web resources for more information on global teams.

WELCOME TO THE WORLD OF GLOBAL TEAMS!

Teams have become the focal points of organizations everywhere, and global teams have become the determinant of global success for todays firms. It is global teams that allow organizations to come together, to create and produce the services and products demanded by global customers, to connect the best ideas and best people for the good of the company. It is the hope of this book that your global teams will become such groups—and that they will be successful in their efforts and enjoyable for their members.

Michael J. Marquardt
Reston, Virginia

Lisa Horvath
Washington, D.C.

About the Authors

Michael J. Marquardt, Ed.D., is professor of global human resource development at George Washington University and president of Global Learning Associates. He has held a number of senior management, training, and marketing positions with organizations such as Grolier, World Center for Development and Training, Association Management, Inc., Overseas Education Fund, TradeTec, and U.S. Office of Personnel Management. Marquardt has trained more than 45,000 managers in eighty-five countries since his first international experience in Spain in 1969. His consulting clients have included Marriott, DuPont, Pentax, Motorola, Nortel, Boeing, United Nations Development Program, Xerox, Nokia, and Singapore Airlines, as well as the governments of Indonesia, Laos, Zambia, Egypt, Turkey, Russia, Jamaica, Honduras, and Swaziland.

Marquardt is author of fourteen books and more than fifty articles in the fields of leadership, learning, globalization, and organizational change. His titles include *Building the Learning Organization* (selected as Book of the Year by the Academy of Human Resource Development), *The Global Advantage, Action Learning in Action, Global Leaders for the 21st Century, Global Human Resource Development,* and *Technology-Based Learning*. He has been a keynote speaker at conferences throughout North America, as well as in Australia, Japan, England, the Philippines, Malaysia, South Africa, Sweden, Singapore, and India.

Marquardt is a recipient of the International Practitioner of the Year Award from the American Society for Training and Development and numerous other awards. He currently serves as a Senior Advisor for the United Nations Staff College in the areas of policy, technology, and learning systems. He is a Fellow of the Academy of Human Resource Development and a cofounder of the Asian Learning Organization Network.

Lisa Horvath, Ph.D., is program chair and assistant professor in human and organizational studies at George Washington University and was formerly associated with the Center for Creative Leadership. She has presented and published on such topics as team performance and training, virtual and global work, and organizational change, and she has consulted to numerous organizations on work group effectiveness and training. Currently she is on leave from George Washington University and is serving as a visiting assistant professor at the Singapore Management University.

Part One

THE CORNERSTONES

Chapter 1

The Power of Global Teams

Leaders around the world are now recognizing the critical importance of global teams as the key to future competitiveness and productivity in today's new network-style global organization. The power of global teams to respond quickly to corporate challenges has become the key to a company's ultimate success in the global marketplace. For example,

- Marriott faced the challenge of quickly integrating the $1 billion Renaissance and New World hotel chain into the Marriott fold. A global team was formed to do a complete assessment of the current status of the new hotels: what brand might fit best, what capital expenditures would be necessary to bring the new hotels up to Marriott standards, and what architectural and interior design modifications were needed. Within thirty days, the global team had successfully developed a strategy and written procedures that enabled all the hotels to attain operational status and add to Marriott's global growth and prestige.

- At Royal Dutch Shell, six global teams meet every week at the Exploration and Production divisions in Houston and the Netherlands to mull over ideas that have been pitched to them by e-mail. The teams (known as GameChangers) have reviewed hundreds of ideas from employees—everything from ways to reduce company paperwork to using laser sensors to discover oil. The results have been outstanding. Of Shell's five top business initiatives in 1999, four emerged from the global GameChanger teams. And now these projects are reaping millions of dollars. One successful initiative engendered by the global virtual teams was Shell's new "Light Touch" oil-discovery method, which helps explorers by sensing hydrocarbon emissions released naturally into the air from underground reserves. This laser technology recently helped locate some 30 million barrels of oil reserves in Gabon.

- Two large pharmaceutical companies, Marion Laboratories and Merrell Dow, with combined sales of over $3 billion and several thousand employees around the world, merged in 1999 to become MMD. Thanks to the efforts of the global team composed of members of the two companies, the merger succeeded and every MMD site improved production levels, lowered costs, and increased speed.

Very few organizations, however, have successfully developed and utilized global teams. Although teams are increasingly seen as essential for global prosperity, they fail far more often than they succeed. A number of obstacles—cultural differences, great distances and time zones, the complexity of global teamworking, language differences, the costs and time involved in arranging face-to-face meetings—have overwhelmed most companies. Thus the building of global teams is the biggest business challenge of the twenty-first century: the sine qua non for global success.

WHAT ARE GLOBAL TEAMS?

Although there are many definitions of global teams, in this book the term refers to a group of people of different nationalities working together on a common project across cultures and time zones for extended periods of time. The global team is expected to achieve an outcome that will either serve a widespread set of customers, solve problems in many areas simultaneously, or have a significant impact on increasing or sustaining the organization's profitability and service. The growing power of technology enables the work of global teams to be done both face-to-face and virtually so that members may work at different times and in different locations as well as in the same time and place. Global teams typically work on projects that are highly complex and have a considerable effect on company objectives.

The emergence of global teams has been caused by the globalization of the world economy—the most significant trend of the times. Globalization has reshaped not only the macro-level aspects of economic life but also the micro-level details of each individual's life. It has created global customers and global corporations. There is an ever-increasing economic interdependence among countries that is caused by numerous joint ventures, strategic alliances, and mergers and acquisitions. More and more companies, whether small or large, young or old, recognize that their choice is between becoming global—and building global teams—or becoming extinct.

THE IMPORTANCE OF TEAMS IN THE NEW CENTURY

Teams have become the basic modus operandi for getting things done. Teams of all types have become the heart and soul of organizational life and productivity. Among a growing host of critical roles, they are being used to manage cross-functional projects, work on the assembly line, reengineer business processes, and develop marketing strategies.

Tom Peters (1992), the noted guru on the future of organizations, sees teams as the foundation for organizational survival for the twenty-first century. He offers the following predictions about the importance of teams and their composition as we enter the new millennium:

- Most of tomorrow's work will be done in project teams. The life span of a project team might be indeterminate or just a few hours. Dynamic but short-lived project configurations will be commonplace.

- Whatever their size—whether they have 200,000 employees or twenty—organizations will be dismantled into fast, learning-efficient teams of four to forty members.

- It will not be uncommon for people to work on four or five project teams in a year—but you might never work twice with the same configuration of colleagues.

- The typical project team will include "outsiders" such as vendors, customers, and distributors.

- Who reports to whom will change over time. You may report to a person for one task while that person reports to you for another task. Thus the ability to lead a group will become an almost universal skill.

- Developing world-class teams with world-class members will be more important than any single business victory.

- Performance appraisals will be based primarily on team skills and success, and they will be done by fellow team members.

- There will be constant reorganizing, restructuring, and reengineering based on endless reconfiguration of project teams.

Teams, like companies, are going global. As Davison and Ward (1999) note, global teams are necessary for creating a company's "sustainable global capability." The increasing complexities of scientific, sociological, and commercial issues demand that people from different cultural backgrounds and different nations collaborate in order to resolve global problems creatively and take advantage of global opportunities.

And why must global teams be the avenue for organizational responses to these challenges? The simple answer is that today's global problems are too complex, require too much speed, and involve too many resources for local teams, much less individual leaders, to resolve. Global teams have the capacity to be much more resourceful and ultimately successful. The power generated by the technology revolution now makes it possible for people to participate in meaningful interaction anywhere and anytime, for groups to spend as much time working apart as together, for people to access and share information as never before.

POWER OF GLOBAL TEAMS

Simply put, companies that have good global teams will blow the competition away. Their power to link and leverage, to move and manipulate

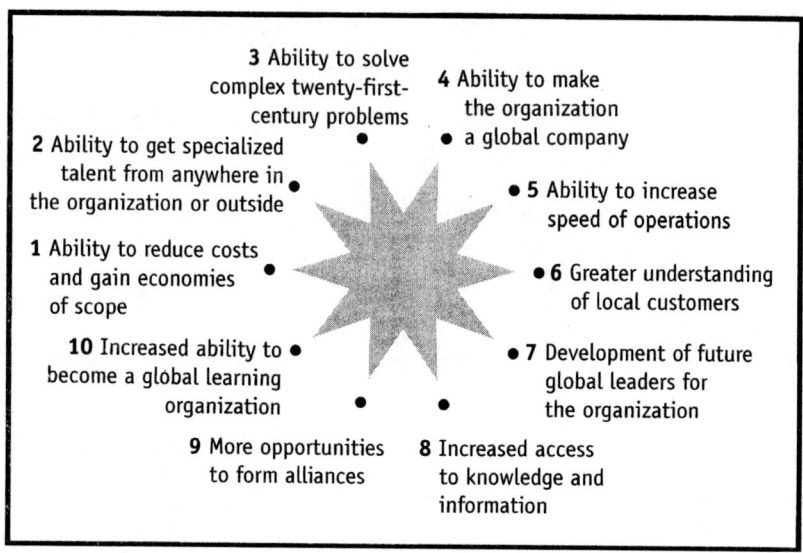

Figure 1 • POWER SOURCES OF GLOBAL TEAMS

resources, to provide superior services and products at low costs will overwhelm competitors who do not use global teams. Global firms with global teams will exponentially increase their competitive edge as they acquire the best workers, produce the best products, and attract the best customers.

Why do global teams have such strength and power? What is the source of their robust capabilities? How do they link and leverage these overwhelming advantages? Let's examine the ten benefits of global teams that have been cited most frequently by global executives and leading global theorists. (See Figure 1.)

Ability to Reduce Costs and Gain Economies of Scope

A primary value of global teams, according to Bartlett and Ghoshal (1998), is to achieve global efficiency through the development of worldwide and regional cost advantages as well as standardization of designs and operations. Although establishing global teams may require additional costs for travel and technology, there are a number of ways in which global teams can reduce costs:

- They can integrate across functions, across boundaries, and across professional areas.
- They can reduce duplication of activities by eliminating and consolidating identical activities.
- They allow for more efficient and focused use of human resources.
- Companies can avoid duplication of effort as global teams develop worldwide best practices and strategies.
- Global teams can develop lower costs, shorter delivery times, and broad assortments of standard products.
- The steep learning and experience benefits gained via global teams can ultimately result in higher productivity and profits.
- Team membership can be composed of high-quality talent at a much lower cost because of the location of members.

COLGATE-PALMOLIVE'S TPM

As Colgate-Palmolive enters the global marketplace, there is increased pressure to reduce costs and standardize products and services for economies of scale and scope. A global team was established four years ago to assure that employees have access to the best worldwide technology and use it properly. As a result of the efforts by the Total Productivity Maintenance (TPM) global team, Colgate now has a global set of tools and standards and is doing quality training to meet those levels. Colgate has also been able to lower costs since less equipment is needed and less waste occurs. A number of approaches have been eliminated that required money being spent on resources and consultants that were no longer needed. Finally, productivity is better organized—which means employees are more inclined to work. Chapter 10 describes the efforts of the TPM global team.

Ability to Get Specialized Talent from Anywhere in the Organization or Outside

Global companies need access to the best people around the world, regardless of nationality, background, or location. These people bring to the organization the experience and learning from their cultures, from their best universities, from their best organizations. Scott Snell et al. (1998) point out that one of the greatest benefits of global teams is the fact that the company's HR department is forced to "seek, motivate and develop superior talent from around the world" (p. 182).

Due to the power of technology, teams can now communicate and work together even though separated by great distances and time. Virtuality and asynchronicity allow an organization to link the best people from within the organization as well as outside. If access to top knowledge and skills leads to greater corporate success, global teams provide that power.

Global firms such as Nokia, Cisco Systems, Microsoft, and General Electric pride themselves on obtaining the highest quality of people from each country in which they operate and putting them on global teams.

Ability to Solve Complex Twenty-first-Century Problems

The twenty-first-century workplace will involve rapidly changing socioeconomic trends and markets, overnight innovation from competitors, mergers across disparate corporate cultures and industries, new distribution channels, and globalization of business. Heifetz and Laurie (1998) make a distinction between twentieth-century problems and those that will be most critical in the new century. They call these technical versus adaptive problems.

Technical problems (twentieth century) are those in which the knowledge needed to solve the problem already exists in a legitimized form or set of procedures. The challenge in solving these problems is to obtain the knowledge and apply it in an efficient and rational way. Technical problems have a linear, logical way of being solved, and there are precedents within the organization or beyond.

Adaptive problems (twenty-first century) are those for which no satisfactory response has been developed and no technical expertise is fully adequate—problems such as handling global mergers or retaining knowledge workers. The challenge is to mobilize the people with the problem to make painful adjustments in their attitudes, work habits, and other aspects of their lives, while at the same time learning their way into the creation of something that does not yet exist. Adaptive problems have no ready solutions. They require people collectively "to apply their intelligence and skills to the work only they can do. The responsibility requires unlearning the habits of a managerial lifetime, new learning to meet challenges where current skills are insufficient, and capacity to explore and understand competing values at stake" (Heifetz and Laurie, 1998, p. 2)

Adaptive challenges are more difficult to define and resolve precisely because they require the effort of people throughout the organization. As the workplace becomes more complex, however, strategic problems will require more than a technical response. Leaders and teams will be faced with learning more adaptive approaches in order to solve problems for which no plan of action has yet been developed and current technical expertise is not fully adequate.

Thus problems will become ever more confusing and difficult to identify, much less solve. And solving problems will no longer be the domain of any single person or leader—we will need to incorporate the information, imagination, perspectives, and talents of many people to find answers to tomorrow's dilemmas. In confronting twenty-first-century problems, organizations will need to create new entities such as global teams that have the internal diversity and complexity required to understand and solve such problems (Schwandt and Marquardt, 2000).

Research by Snell et al. (1998) shows that global teams are much more effective than homogeneous teams when the key challenge facing a group is to generate a broad array of ideas that will lead to a new and more powerful solution than has been considered previously. This occurs because global teams, being located in and working with numerous cultures, are able to synergize the strengths of differing cultures. In fact, their diversity can be a primary source of new ideas when innovation and creativity are needed.

The complex problems of the global marketplace require new ways of thinking and fresh ideas. Mobilizing the energy and the differences of various cultures can lead to multiple perspectives and a wider range of approaches to problems and challenges.

MARRIOTT'S GLOBAL TEAMS

Marriott recently used global teams to resolve two critical adaptive problems it was facing. The first problem was worldwide preparedness for Y2K. As one can imagine, preparing for Y2K on a worldwide basis was a tremendous challenge. A Marriott global team met for crisis simulation on an annual basis before 1999 and on a quarterly basis in 1999. A wide array of urgent contingencies needed to be developed, including:

- Full assessment of hotel, country, and city preparedness
- Preparing for the well-being of guests in every country so there would be a safe haven in case of catastrophe
- Handling elevators, fire protection, water, electrical supply, government services (police and army), supply chains, food, refrigeration, laundry
- Establishing an Iridium phone system for call-crisis centers in Los Angeles, Hong Kong, Frankfurt, and Washington, D.C.
- Interactive participation with the general managers of each hotel
- Media people trained for crisis communication

The second problem was globalizing Marriott management brands. Marriott has a number of different hotel brands—Ritz, JW Marriott, Courtyard by Marriott—each needing global standards (reservations, sales, and the like) as well as localized or regionalized touches while maintaining the brand requirements of the local owner (Courtyard in China with nine-course meals, a 57 Ritz in a palace in Berlin). A global team quickly analyzed and developed worldwide standards and implementation procedures.

In Chapter 5, we describe in more detail how and why Marriott uses global teams.

Ability to Make the Organization a Global Company

Companies around the world are rushing to globalize—recognizing that globalization provides significant competitive and comparative advantages. Most organizations, however, still think and operate in an international (or at best a multinational) mode. They do not know how to link and leverage resources on a single worldwide basis, how to operate without borders, how to go global.

Global teams are "at the heart of the globalization process" (Snow et al., 1996). Global leaders see the development of global teams as a key to launching and managing the transition to global status. Establishing a global presence and being seen with global players can occur quickly with global teams.

What's more, creating global teams forces the organization to begin operating in a global fashion. The existence of global teams helps group members develop a global mind-set and a greater appreciation of cultures. It enables people within the organization to think and see the world globally, to be more open to exchanging ideas across borders, and to break down provincial ways of thinking.

ARTHUR ANDERSEN'S GLOBAL TEAMS

Working on global teams at Arthur Andersen is a regular part of the worklife of the more than 100,000 employees located in nearly ninety countries. One of their most successful global team efforts was the virtual team that developed the performance support tool for Andersen Worldwide's North American Payroll System (NAPS). The firm chose to use a global team and a distance development approach for the following reasons:

- To maximize the diversity of cultural and geographic viewpoints
- To ensure that materials were developed with the end-user perspective
- To lower the cost of development
- To reduce the impact on the developer's daily operations—thus lessening the impact on their offices
- To be better able to use expertise dispersed across a broad geographic area

Ability to Increase Speed of Operations

With team members located in different time zones around the world, there is now the possibility of around-the-clock efforts. Team members in Singapore may work on a project for eight hours and then transmit their efforts to team members in London—who, in turn, after another eight hours send their work to team members in Los Angeles. Team members at each site can tap the resources available in their region of the world during the normal working hours of that region.

IBM'S GLOBAL TEAMS

IBM created a five-site, five-country global team that would work around the clock for the purpose of developing the VisualAge application development environment. The efforts of the JavaBeans teams (so called because they were working on the small components—or beans—of the application) resulted in significant benefits to IBM. The cost of the offshore sites was 10 percent of such activities in North America. The teams were able to reduce time-to-market from three months to less than a month. Moreover, IBM was able to create a strong presence in each of the emerging markets in which team members were operating as well as develop a strong base of computer expertise. (See Chapter 7 for more specifics on the work of the JavaBeans teams.)

Greater Understanding of Local Customers

The most successful global corporations are those that are sensitive to local situations—those that have "glocalized" (that is, they have a global reach but a local touch). Such companies appreciate the value of face-to-face interactions to gather information. By building stronger relationships with suppliers and customers, they are designing more culturally sensitive products and processes.

Since members of global teams are located at the various manufacturing and marketing sites of the company, decisions will be made by people who have greater proximity to—and hence understanding of—the organization's customers. Local people who serve as members of the global team bring an understanding of workers and customers from their part of the world: buying habits, cultural practices, motivational factors that work, management attributes that are effective in the local environment.

GLOBAL TEAMS

The increased creativity and flexibility generated by multicultural teams can prove invaluable in addressing culturally distinct clients and environments. Thus global teams are able to create global strategies that are more sensitive to local requirements and the demands of a country's market structure, consumer preferences, and political and legal systems.

PFIZER'S GLOBAL TEAMS

Pfizer has launched twenty new global teams in Canada, Latin America, Asia, Europe, and Africa/Middle East to work on product issues and improve customer service. Plans are under way to establish a Center of Excellence for Global Teams to expand the company's use of global teams and discover new ways to cross-pollinate and leverage resources across country borders and organizational functions. As a result, Pfizer is successfully changing both its infrastructure and its institutional culture. Chapter 8 presents Pfizer's journey to build these successful global teams.

Development of Future Global Leaders for the Organization

Global teams provide a wonderful opportunity to develop the people needed by global companies. As Snell et al. (1998) note: "If a company wishes to select, retain, and develop exceptional employees in multiple parts of the world—particularly in professional and managerial ranks—then it must establish vehicles by which the employees' current talents are fully tapped, as well as ways to enhance the employees' capacity for making future contributions to the company" (p. 200).

This is especially important for employees located at sites away from headquarters. Few things are as frustrating to a talented, ambitious midlevel manager as being treated as a "local nobody"—allowed to make contributions only in his or her own country operation while matters of global significance and important strategic or innovative endeavors remain the purview of people in the headquarters country. With the presence of global teams, however, the company greatly enhances the opportunity to utilize and develop these talented people. Employees with demonstrated aptitudes for working in global teams can get the opportunity of working on companywide issues and be seen as future shining stars. Indeed, Hamel and Prahalad (1994) believe that the successful use of global teams in building a company's HR capability will be among the critical strengths needed for companies to prosper in the new century.

ERNST & YOUNG'S GLOBAL TEAMS

Ernst & Young is one of many companies (others include General Electric, Unilever, General Motors, and Marriott) where membership in global teams is being seen as a key tool in building future global leaders. Like many global consulting firms, Ernst & Young needs to attract, develop, and retain high-performing leaders. A global team was recently formed to look at best practices across countries in the Ernst & Young community in order to identify recruiting and retention strategies, global procedures, and the reasons why people stay or leave. Members of such teams quickly become new global leaders for Ernst & Young. In Chapter 5 we explore in more detail the efforts of global teams at Ernst & Young.

Increased Access to Knowledge and Information

Information and knowledge have become *the* competitive advantage of an organization (Sveiby, 1997; Stewart, 1997). According to leading futurists and business leaders, we have entered the *knowledge era*; the new economy is a *knowledge economy*. Knowledge provides the key raw material for wealth creation and is the fountain of organizational and personal power. Simply put: Knowledge has become more important for organizations than financial resources, market position, technology, or any other company asset. Knowledge is seen as the main resource used in performing work in an organization. The organization's traditions, culture, technology, operations, systems, and procedures are all based on knowledge and expertise.

The organization with the most information (about new technologies, customers, sources of best employees, political happenings, and so forth) will generally be able to make better decisions and produce better products and services. Thus global companies deliberately establish a presence via global teams in countries that are a major source of industry innovation and have prestigious, high-quality universities. Global companies seek ways to be located near Cambridge or Silicon Valley or Singapore so they can gain direct access to the many sources of innovation present in these locations. Here they will have more opportunities—to seek out face-to-face contacts with university researchers, to participate in technical and professional conferences, to acquire quicker access to publications (many scientific journals are published only in Japanese, for example, and circulate little outside the country), and to hire the best local minds.

GENERAL MOTORS UNIVERSITY'S GLOBAL TEAM

General Motors University (GMU) is assisted by a global team with members from Singapore, Zurich, São Paulo, and Detroit, thus allowing its members to be knowledgeable about the latest training and learning resources in all parts of the world. The global team has achieved a number of successes, including the globalization of all courseware. A number of courses have been made available on the GMU Intranet both in English and the local language. A global sourcing process has been developed that includes bidding, soliciting, and negotiation. Training has moved from a North American focus to a global focus, and an increasing number of worldwide distance learning programs are available. In Chapter 4 we illustrate the activities of the GMU global team.

More Opportunities to Form Alliances

Members of global teams may be composed of employees of other organizations—particularly, partner companies who are involved in specific activities of the organization. Global companies with their global teams have greater choices for alliances and partnerships as well as becoming more attractive to prospective suitors. Global teams can create opportunities to extend each partner's global reach while at the same time contributing to each partner's local competence.

The presence of local team members offer greater opportunities to compete in the local market for these partners due to convenience and proximity and greater levels of trust. Such global alliances provide innumerable advantages for the global company: combining of physical and human resources; sharing of capital, equipment, and information; easier and greater market access; and more. As we shall see, Whirlpool, Nokia, Glaxo-Wellcome, Boeing, and Alcoa are some of the companies that use global teams as a key strategy for involving people from other firms in order to expand corporate capabilities and market opportunities.

Increased Ability to Become a Global Learning Organization

Global companies have greater requirements, opportunities, and resources for acquiring, creating, storing, transferring, applying, and testing knowledge—the essence of a learning organization. The synergy of culture, the demand of global customers, and the challenges of global competition compel the organization to learn faster and continuously. Every employee needs to be a learner; every occasion needs to be a learning opportunity. Learning is necessary throughout the organization and is aligned with the business goals of the company. High-quality learners, customer demand for constant innovation, and cultural diversity all push global companies into becoming learning organizations.

Global teams offer the richest resource for organizations wishing to learn how to gather, store, utilize, and distribute knowledge about the global market to different people in all parts of the company—in short, wishing to become a global learning organization (Marquardt and Reynolds, 1994).

BP'S GLOBAL TEAMS

BP (see Chapter 7) uses global teams not only to increase incremental efficiencies but also to improve how work is done in the organization. The company is using teams to build its knowledge base and develop a repository of solutions to frequently encountered problems. The company believes that the combination of technology and coaching will lead to an ever more collaborative culture of executive decision making across the organization—and ultimately to the creation of a global learning organization.

CHALLENGES FOR GLOBAL TEAMS

The impact and value of these ten sources of power attained via global teams should compel every organization to establish global teams systematically and quickly. The future success of the company—if not its survival—will depend on building effective global teams. But creating and maintaining global teams is a complex task that requires the overcoming of significant challenges—challenges that we explore in Chapter 2.

Chapter 2

Five Challenges Facing Global Teams

Although an enormous amount of power may be accrued through global teams, there are also tremendous challenges—challenges that sometimes prove too difficult for organizations to overcome. As a result, many organizations end up with global teams that are ineffective and drain resources and energy rather than solve problems and generate success. On most global teams, frustrations outnumber successes. Global executives, all too frequently, recount stories of setbacks caused by global teams, strategic plans that have suffered, careers that got derailed, projects that have taken so long that the competition took over the market.

What are these difficulties? Why do they seem so formidable? What are the underlying factors causing these frustrations? In this chapter we explore the five major challenges that can cause the downfall of global teams (see Figure 2) and discuss the elements that make these challenges so tough. Later in the chapter we present the GlobalTeams Model—a model that, when implemented, will enable companies and teams to overcome these five challenges:

- Managing cultural diversity, differences, and conflicts
- Handling geographic distances, dispersion, and despair
- Dealing with coordination and control issues
- Maintaining communication richness over distances
- Developing and maintaining teamness

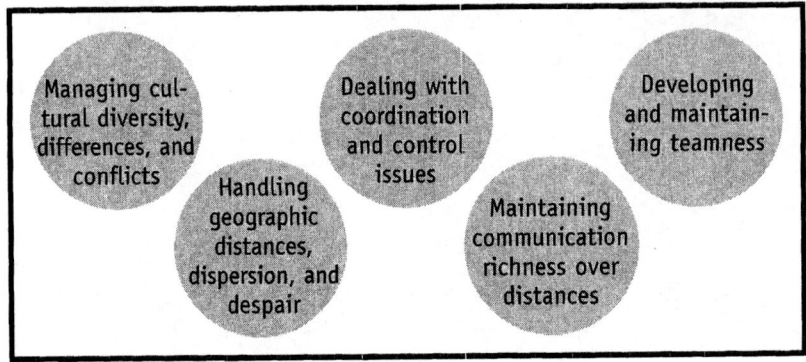

Figure 2 • CHALLENGES OF GLOBAL TEAMS

MANAGING CULTURAL DIVERSITY, DIFFERENCES, AND CONFLICTS

Managing cultural diversity is the challenge that prevents most global teams from being effective. Why? Because most of us simply do not realize the presence of culture (like fish not realizing they are in water), much less understand it. Simply defined, culture is a way of thinking, acting, and living that is shared by members of a group and passed on from older members to new ones. Culture consciously and subconsciously shapes the group's and each member's values, assumptions, perceptions, and behavior. It provides the group with systematic guidelines for how they should conduct their thinking, their actions, their rituals, and their business (Marquardt and Engel, 1993).

Culture represents a challenge to global teams because cultures are different and thus create differences. Cultures cause members to see reality very differently. Each of us believes, of course, that our perception of reality is the correct one. Culture, which we begin learning almost at birth, leads us to believe that our way of thinking, acting, and doing things is the only rational way of thinking, acting, and doing. But to impose our way of seeing things and doing things will seem strange, ridiculous, or unfair to someone of another culture.

Thus a host of acrimonious and seemingly unsolvable problems may arise because of mistrust, miscommunication, and lack of cohesion caused by cultural differences. The challenge of global teams is to achieve a balance between fostering the healthy clash of ideas while controlling cultural differences among team members.

Let's take a brief look at some of the key cultural differences that affect how people work in teams. First we need to be aware of the fact that Western and non-Western cultures have created a number of clear distinctions in the way people think and act, how they perceive the world around them, and how they live their lives. The following list suggests a few of these differences:

Western Values	Non-Western Values
Individualism	Collectivism
Achievement	Modesty
Equality	Hierarchy
Winning	Collaboration
Guilt (internal self-control)	Shame (external control)
Pride	Saving face
Respect for results	Respect for status
Respect for competence	Respect for elders
Time is money	Time is life
Action/doing	Being/acceptance
Systematic	Humanistic
Tasks	Relationships
Informal	Formal
Assertiveness	Indirectness
Future/change	Past/tradition
Control	Fate
Linear	Holistic
Verbal	Nonverbal

Naturally, these different ways of thinking and acting affect how team members from different cultures participate in various group activities and process.

Leadership Roles and Expectations

Western managers are taught to employ a participative, democratic style of leadership. Everyone is encouraged to express their opinion in order for the goals of the organization to be achieved. Westerners prefer the impersonal authority of mutually agreed-upon goals and objectives rather than the arbitrary power of a superior. Disagreeing with a manager is not uncommon, and followers are expected to take the initiative.

Efforts are made to minimize inequality through legal and political means. Our organizations tend to be flatter, and power is decentralized. Managers must earn our respect, as it is not automatically granted.

These roles and expectations relative to leaders are less common elsewhere in the world where leadership may be more hierarchical. Managers are expected to make decisions rather than work out the problem with subordinates. Work may not easily bypass a chain of command. There may be a clear hierarchy based on status—age, sex, family, title—that discourages lower-level workers from airing their views freely lest they be considered disrespectful or be viewed as "the nail that sticks out." Power and authority are centralized and organizational structure—in terms of highly demarcated levels—is tightly controlled. A leader may need to act in a certain formal way or otherwise lose credibility.

Individualism and Groups

Based on a number of cultural research studies (Hofstede, 1991; Trompenaars, 1994), the United States is the most individualistic culture in the world. The rights of individuals are often seen as being more important than the common good of the community. Americans place a high value on independence; obligations between people are few; tasks are valued over relationships.

Most cultures of the world, however, are more group-oriented or collectivist. People in these cultures tend to subordinate individual interests for the good of the group. Groups protect their members in exchange for loyalty and obedience. Personal identity is based on the social network to which you belong. Thus harmony is more valued than speaking your mind or being "brutally honest."

Communications

Communication among group members may be seen and practiced quite differently because of cultural upbringing. One such area is a person's communication style.

An *expressive* communication style, as found in the cultures of Latin America, the Middle East, and Southern and Eastern Europe, is considered a highly valued art form. People from these countries are less concerned with the precision of communication than with the establish-

rooted in courtesy and respect. Here are some examples of indirect communication strategies:

- *Mediation:* A third person is used as a go-between.
- *Refraction:* Statements intended for person A are made to person B while person A is present.
- *Covert revelation:* A person portrays himself as a messenger for someone else or allows notes to fall into the hands of another party.
- *Correspondence:* Written communication can be used to avoid direct interaction.
- *Anticipation:* Sometimes it helps to be understated and unobtrusive in order to accommodate the unspoken needs of the other person.
- *Ritual:* Rituals help to maintain control of an uncertain situation.

Perspectives on Time

Different cultures have widely differing perspectives regarding the use of time—in terms of importance, in terms of focus, and in terms of relating to the past, present, and future. In the United States, time is very important. "Time is money" and "don't waste time" are dictums we hear from early childhood onward. Time is seen by Americans as a precious resource they must control: There is a sense of punctuality, deadlines, and urgency. Meetings begin on time and schedules are taken seriously.

This attitude toward punctuality is less prevalent in many other societies—especially in Latin America and the Middle East, where time is not worshiped in the same way. In these regions of the world, relationships are more important than promptness. And fully understanding and discussing an interesting point is more important than staying on schedule. Time is more fluid; it can wait; and "soon" may mean three months or when we are ready. Thus delays are expected.

People's focus on time also varies across cultures. It can be viewed as *polychronic* (multifocused) or *monochronic* (single-focused). Monochronic cultures like the United States prefer to concentrate on one task at a time. Plans and schedules tend to be detailed, followed quite strictly, and changed infrequently. In multifocused cultures, people feel comfortable undertaking simultaneous tasks with a high commitment to relationship building rather than just task completion or meeting arbitrary deadlines. Many people and activities may be occurring at the same time.

Cultures also have varying degrees of emphasis on the past, the present, and the future. Tradition-oriented cultures use the past as a context for evaluating the present; plans need to fit with what has happened previously; leaders, teams, and individuals should follow precedents that fit well-established criteria and demonstrate loyalty and adherence to accepted norms, policies, and procedures. Present-focused cultures take care of today, and tomorrow will take care of itself. There is a greater emphasis on short-term plans and a focusing on current goals. Future-oriented cultures have a greater willingness to trade short-term gains for long-term results.

Flexibility and Control

People of various cultures differ in their willingness to be flexible and in their ability to accept uncertainty. Many cultures value certainty and order since they have a need for predictability and cannot tolerate ambiguity. They seek clear roles and responsibilities as well as work processes that are precise and consistent.

Flexible cultures, on the other hand, are more tolerant of unknown situations, people, and ideas. They are more tolerant of deviations from the norm and more willing to take risks. What works is what counts. These cultures show a preference for broad guidelines rather than specific methodologies. Thus job and task descriptions are broadly interpreted. The leader's role is to provide general direction and vision, and let the others determine the ways to implement them.

Motivation

What motivates people as team members differs significantly from culture to culture. How we work as a team may vary from being very competitive to being cooperative. *Competitive* cultures emphasize being assertive and focus on results, success, and achievements especially as they relate to tasks and rewards. Work is highly valued; it determines one's worth and importance. *Cooperative* cultures place a high value on consensual decision making. Employees are hired, not only for their skills, but also for their ability to fit into the group, promote its shared values, facilitate communication, demonstrate loyalty, and contribute to the overall work environment.

Tensions Generated by Cultural Differences

In light of all these cultural differences, it's clear that global teams will have to work to get all their diverse members to agree on global ways of behaving. Leaders will be challenged indeed to gain consensus on team goals and processes from a group that starts with a range of goals and processes.

A major challenge, then, of global teams is: How do we build trust among team members from different countries, even in different organizations? How can we get them to share information, become motivated, work collaboratively, and get things done on time when they come from diverse functional, corporate, and national cultures, many of which clash with one another?

When establishing and working with global teams, it's absolutely critical to recognize these cultural differences. They have an impact on every activity of every team. Some of these values and behavior may need to be changed. Some may need to be synergized by building something better with the differences—what Devereaux and Johansen (1994) call a "third way." Throughout the remaining chapters of this book, especially in Chapter 6, we will be examining strategies and ideas to overcome this major challenge.

HANDLING GEOGRAPHIC DISTANCES, DISPERSION, AND DESPAIR

The second major difficulty in working with global teams is how to handle physical and psychological separation caused by geographic distance. Although technology enables organizations to be both centralized and decentralized, there are still numerous limitations due to limited face-to-face contact among members of the team and between the team and its outside links.

In many cultures, the personal contact is essential for the transaction of important business or for any progress in partnerships and promotions. Distance can cause people to feel cut off, out of the loop, or even insignificant. Headquarters culture is often misunderstood or denigrated from afar.

Geographic distance has a direct impact on all forms of communications among team members. Distance is an impediment to building relationships of trust. As Charles Handy (1995) states: "Trust needs touch." While co-located global team members can more easily build trust through formal and informal face-to-face meetings, even then trust takes time to develop. Distance obviously makes building trust and good communications much more difficult as people tend to be more constrained in their personal interactions. Co-located teams are less likely to squabble since co-location usually increases trust and reduces miscommunication. The shorter timelines of co-located projects provide the opportunity to give feedback quickly.

Distance also affects coordination and control. Problem solving is more difficult as the team has a hard time understanding each other's styles of decision making. What's more, it becomes much harder to develop cohesiveness—to share a common vision of the team's work and its products.

Most media are linear. A linear format may be appropriate for certain types of information sharing, such as logical stream-progress reports, data, and logistical information. But linear modes cannot communicate the collage of information you encounter by walking into another person's office face-to-face. Managing from a distance results in managing by charts rather than by walking about.

And if the communications format is less context-rich, some cultures will find it extremely uncomfortable. Relying on electronic communication that strips everything but the message may leave too much room for inference. High-context cultures are less comfortable interacting from a distance.

Working on remote global teams can also cause people to feel isolated. What's more, the constant traveling and absences demanded by team activities can be demoralizing and harm family life. Global teams may be operating twenty-four hours a day around the world. Important decisions may need to be taken at 2:00 A.M. your time. Workdays in some countries (Saturdays and Sundays in the Arabian Gulf Region) may be days you'd like to spend with your family. Poorly planned and supported global teams can quickly burn out their members.

Asynchronous communications tend to exacerbate the problem. When members have no overlap of working hours for voice or video conversations, one side always has to compromise.

Thomas Allen (1997), who developed a correlation between distance and communication, discovered that communication drops precipitously when offices are far away from one another (the out-of-sight, out-of-mind syndrome). The informal, oral communication created by distance tends to promote sloppiness in documentation and procedures—such as passing along a half-finished task with the tacit understanding that it will be fixed and documented later. And there is an inclination toward inbreeding, groupthink, and other group pathologies.

In summary, the distance and dispersion challenge in establishing global teams revolves around the issues of integration and separation, collaboration and necessary independence, inclusion and exclusion, everywhere and at the same time.

DEALING WITH COORDINATION AND CONTROL ISSUES

Coordination (the integration of tasks and organizational units so that the team's efforts contribute to the overall objectives) and control (the process of adhering to goals, policies, or standards) are even more important for global teams than for regular organizational teams. Yet the difficulties and challenges are even greater because of the greater complexities caused by cultural, linguistic, and technological issues (Carmel, 1999).

Dispersed teams create burdens on coordination and control mechanisms—primarily the informal ones. Because of distance, management cannot peek around the cubicle wall or bring the team together informally. Because of time differences, managers cannot make a quick phone call to check up, direct activities, or provide advice.

As a result of the distance and team members' different cultural patterns, there is an increased potential for conflict as well as an unwillingness to accept coordination and control. People can also feel torn between loyalty to the global team and loyalty to their local manager. Thus there's a delicate balance between avoiding duplication and inefficiencies and needing to allow autonomy of innovation.

The complexity of coordinating work increases as the interdependence within and between teams increases and the task is difficult, new, or uncertain. All of these factors are common with global teams. James Thompson has identified three types of interdependence and proposes general coordination mechanisms for each: *pooled interdependence* can be coordinated by standardization; *sequential interdependence* can be coordinated by plan; *reciprocal interdependence* needs to be coordinated by mutual adjustment (Carmel, 1999).

Another factor that makes coordination and control more difficult is the large size of many global teams. Global teams in multiple sites are generally larger per task than co-located teams. The more people and the more roles involved, the more challenging the coordinating/control issues.

A final element of the coordination/control challenge relates to the management and followership styles of the organization and team members. Different cultures have different protocols and action chains for reporting to managers, especially foreign managers. Managers who usually work with people of their own culture may not understand how other cultures accept direction.

MAINTAINING COMMUNICATION RICHNESS OVER DISTANCES

Clear, effective communication is absolutely essential for global teams to succeed. Yet much of this communication may need to occur indirectly (people communicating at different times to each other from different places)—which means that the "richness of context" is missing. What do we mean by communications context?

Communications can range from high context to low context, and different cultures communicate differently because of a need for context. *High-context* (or rich-context) cultures have the ability to share experience and make certain things understood without needing to state them explicitly. Rules for speaking and behaving are implicit in the context. In such cultures, a great deal of contextual information is needed about a person or a company before business can be transacted. Communication of meaning is transmitted not just in words. It also relies on group understanding of voice tone, body language, facial expressions, eye contact, speech patterns, use of silence, past interactions, status, and common friends. Meaning tends to be implicit rather than direct, and it is less literal. In various Asian cultures, for example, a "yes" may mean yes, maybe, I don't know, if you say so, or even "no" (determined by the level of nonenthusiasm). The precise meaning depends on the context, not just the words. Silence designates thought, not disengagement. Rushing to fill a silence may be considered pushy, impulsive, or even emotional. Background, family, political and social connections, philosophical beliefs, affiliations, experience—all are important.

Team members from high-context cultures with their myriad non-verbal cues can convey far more meaning than the literal words of a message. In such high-context cultures, business transactions are ritualized and the style in which the rituals are carried out matters more than the words. A high value is placed on face-to-face interactions; after-hours socialization is almost a daily occurrence. Global teams that depend on low-context communication technologies to replace context-rich forms of human interaction unwittingly place the members of high-context cultures at a disadvantage.

Low-context cultures, on the other hand, stress the exchange of facts and information. The message is more important than the medium. Information is given primarily in words, and meaning is expressed explicitly. America's task-centered business, which tends to be impersonal, is a good example of low-context communications. Relatively little information is needed about a person or a company before business can be transacted. Trust and compatibility are not major considerations when doing business. Meaning is communicated directly and explicitly, and the words are the most important carriers of meaning. The primary function of communication in low-context cultures is to exchange information, facts, and opinions. Performance appraisals, for example, are impersonal and direct. In such cultures, a videoconference or an e-mail is usually accepted as an efficient substitute for face-to-face meeting.

Technology, although very powerful and helpful to global teams, is limited in its ability to convey context. It does not allow people to understand each other easily. In addition, low-income countries are more likely to have poor access to the technology that is being used.

From a distance, contextual information about the various pressures pulling at team members is hard to decipher. Developing sensitivity to others' time and responsibilities is almost impossible. When there are constraints, we tend to focus on the work at hand.

Simple and instantaneous long-distance communication increases the potential for misunderstanding by making the need for cultural adjustment less obvious. Miscommunication can easily occur from not having enough contextual information or from reading communications incorrectly. This is even more vexing to handle if multiple groups are involved.

In most cultures, teams and individuals prefer to do their tasks via face-to-face communication since it is much richer in context. When we channel communication into an electronic form, the communication is degraded because we lose some richness. In some cases, using technology for communications may actually be counterproductive in cross-cultural business settings. Figure 3 shows how the various means of communications provide context or lack rich context.

Few global companies have grappled with the context challenge with much success; most don't even recognize its existence. Many of us are simply unaware of the tremendous amount of relevant, needed information we casually obtain from our work environment. Communications, both text and context, are absolutely important to global teams. Nonverbal communication is especially critical. Why? Because only part of the message we communicate is strictly in the explicit text that we transmit. A substantial portion—up to 80 percent—is nonverbal and implicit, consisting of body language such as gestures, facial expression, emotion, and our location in the room. And for many cultures, this nonverbal context is much more important for communicating in an effective manner.

As a result, we have trouble getting accurate information from distant sites, especially the bad news. And in many cultures—in Asia, for example—people have great difficulty in telling us that things are going

```
High Contextual Interaction
  ↑    Regular mail
       Express mail
       Electronic mail
       Fax
       Voice mail
       Electronic chat
       One-way broadcast audio
       One-way broadcast video
       Telephone
       Live board with point-to-point audio
       One-way broadcast video with audio back channel
       Point-to-point video conference
       Virtual reality meeting
  ↓    Face-to-face meeting
Low Contextual Interaction
```

Figure 3 • LEVELS OF CONTEXTUAL INTERACTION
Source: Adapted from Carmel (1999)

wrong. Global teams thus have to build a strong communications context or suffer the consequences of weak team interactions and less-than-satisfactory team results.

DEVELOPING AND MAINTAINING TEAMNESS

For most of us, a team means co-location, cultural homogeneity, trust, common communication patterns, a relatively small number of members, and, most important, cohesion. We recognize that teams are, in many ways, fragile social units that can easily crumble. So when you add the burdens of distance, time zone differences, and cross-cultural differences to teams, most lose their "teamness"—the synergistic effect that makes it successful as a cohesive unit (Carmel, 1999, p. 42).

Sharing a common understanding of team goals and actions is difficult enough in single-culture situations. But in global, multicultural settings, one cannot be sure that all members even understand what a team is. Some cultures have little experience of teamwork; some languages even lack a word for team. "Team" means something different to Peruvians and to Pakistanis—who in turn will see it differently from Nigerians and Nepalese. Expectations of leadership, peer relations, group planning and decision making, information sharing, styles of communication, as we noted above, all operate on different cultural assumptions. Some cultures may value the harmony and the welfare of the group above their own personal ambition—collectivist cultures, for example—and within these cultures teams will naturally form into more cohesive units because people are more inclined to find meaning in team membership. People of other cultures may place little value on groups, other than as a means of gaining individual success.

Global teams often work virtually—using technology for communicating and decision making rather than doing it face-to-face. This lack of a personal touch affects team members' relationships and whether they really feel part of a team.

What's more, the geographic and cultural separation means that the key ingredient of trust takes longer to emerge. Thus the important teamness element of "team culture" is much more difficult to build. Yet global teams do not usually have time to get to know each other well as they must quickly focus on tasks.

Group cohesion is also much more difficult for global teams to achieve for a multitude of reasons: members not being able to trust each other due to excessive cultural stereotyping, more "in-group conversations" among those of the same culture, and incidents of miscommunication due to language. Team members may not be as relaxed with people from another culture.

Finally, global teams are often much larger than co-located teams—up to fifty members with five to ten at several sites—further weakening teamness since the intimacy caused by smallness is lost. And the larger the group, the greater the complexity of communication links.

FIVE CHALLENGES FACING GLOBAL TEAMS

CHALLENGES FACED BY ERNST & YOUNG'S GLOBAL HR TEAM

Laurie Friedman

Ernst & Young's Global HR Team is composed of twenty-two members from eleven countries. Although all members of the team work for the same company, each member thinks in a different way and handles recruitment and retention issues differently.

Communicating across space and time has presented major challenges for the team. E-mail is the primary tool used for communication, and initially there were no face-to-face meetings. Language differences are a major problem. Although everyone speaks English, there are cultural and vocabulary differences.

Time zone issues present another obstacle the team had to overcome. The team manager has to try to accommodate and schedule conference calls around the needs of each member country. Most conference calls are held in the early morning, but the project manager quickly discovered that Europeans do not generally work as late as Americans. There were also a number of equipment obstacles that created unique challenges for the global team. With so many countries participating across the globe, there were phone line glitches and static.

Cultural differences were discovered as the tasks of the team members became more specific. The European countries tended to be more paper-based and always wanted hard copies express-mailed to them. They did not want to be online. Since most of the team members in Europe tended to travel a great deal, they preferred paper copies to read on their travels.

The European countries tend to communicate in a very direct way. The team leader quickly learned she had to adjust her management and communication style. She needed to step back and reflect on her writing and speaking approach—to be much more careful to avoid ambiguous language. E-mails had to be constructed to be "very direct, very friendly, and very polite."

An example of how cultural differences can affect a project's outcome occurred around the issue of personnel. Italy has different laws and regulations regarding the sharing of personal information on employees. Since this project requires personal data in order to assess entry information, the members from Italy were uncomfortable with the information they had to reveal. Other members of the global team were unaware of this difference, however, so several strategies had to be reconsidered and changed. Italian concerns centered on the inordinate amount of work required in gathering the data. Initially they thought it would be "too cumbersome" a project. Once the problem was diagnosed and the project scope declared "fairly simple to achieve," they were willing to participate actively in the project. The project manager and the team worked together to develop a greater understanding of Italy's contextual issues and unique challenges. Through this joint exploration, Italy's needs and concerns were uncovered and a better relationship was fostered.

OVERCOMING THE FIVE GLOBAL CHALLENGES

Each of these five forces significantly affects the initial creation and life-long capability of global workteams. As a result of the complexities unique to global teams, organizations and teams have to pay as much attention to how they are approaching a task as to what the task itself involves (Davison and Ward, 1999, p. 21). This demands not only time and expense but also a considerable change of mind-set and refocusing of many organizational policies and processes. Global teams will face ever more complex problems and perplexing opportunities, yet they will have less time to prepare and develop themselves to manage these challenges. Worksheet 1 at the end of this chapter provides a framework for readers to assess their global team's readiness for the five challenges.

Organizations are seeking a systematic framework and strategic guidelines to overcome these challenges. Based on the extensive experience and research of leaders in the fields of globalization and group theory, we have developed the GlobalTeams Model. The GlobalTeams Model has three levels and nine components (Figure 4).

Outer Circle: Team Boundaries and Bridges

Global teams must first be concerned with developing a cohesive boundary around the team and with each other. By definition, global teams have many boundaries—including time, space, and nationality—that

FIVE CHALLENGES FACING GLOBAL TEAMS

Boundaries and Bridges

Cultural and Technological Foundations

HR Alignments
6. Selection and development
7. Facilitation
8. Measurement and feedback
9. Rewards

4. Global and cultural environment
5. Technological infrastructure

1. Leadership
2. Vision, goals, and boundaries
3. Trust and norms

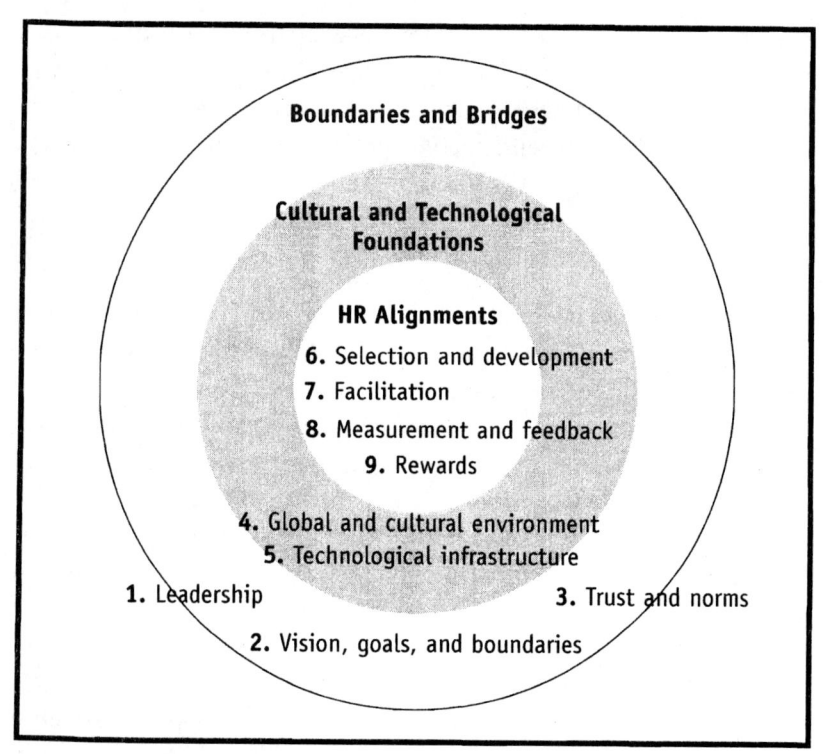

Figure 4 • GLOBALTEAMS MODEL

separate their members from one another. To build a successful global team the key is to create psychological and physical boundaries around the team, rather than around members of the team, giving the team a sense of who they are and what they stand for. The goal is to create a bridge between members and allow the group to work effectively and comfortably with one another. The team boundaries allow the group to distinguish themselves from the outside environment. This is accomplished through (1) developing effective *leadership*, (2) creating a shared team *vision* and identity with clear *goals* and *boundaries*, and (3) building swift *trust* based on shared *norms*.

Middle Circle: Cultural and Technological Foundations

In developing, managing, and sustaining high-performance global teams it is necessary to start with laying the organizational foundation for global work. The first question to ask is this: How can the organization provide the structure and support for global teams? Two critical aspects of this organizational structure are (4) a *global and cultural environment* conducive to supporting diversity and (5) a *technological infrastructure* that is compatible, efficient, and comprehensive so that it enables people to communicate effectively with one another.

Inner Circle: HR Alignments

Once the global team has developed an identity and created bonds between members, it is necessary to align the human resource practices in order to sustain their high performance. Working in a global environment is different from working in a traditional setting. It requires organizational policies, practices, and systems that support collective work. To produce effective global teams, one must align the HR policy and programs with a globally diverse and distributed population. This includes: (6) harnessing cultural, interpersonal, and technical expertise through *selection and development* of the global team members, (7) providing *facilitation* to optimize communication and productivity, (8) incorporating *measurement and feedback* systems tailor-made for global teams, and (9) designing team-oriented *rewards* and performance appraisal systems.

When the nine components of the GlobalTeams Model are integrated and incorporated, companies will have the power to build and maintain effective, enjoyable, and successful global teams. Let's begin the journey!

FIVE CHALLENGES FACING GLOBAL TEAMS

Assessing Challenges in Establishing and Maintaining Global Teams

Directions: This assessment will allow your team to analyze how they have met the challenge of developing a global team. For each statement select the box that represents your experience of the team: 1 = strongly disagree; 2 = disagree; 3 = neither agree or disagree; 4 = agree; 5 = strongly agree. Then add up your score. The scoring key is located at the end of the assessment.

ASSESSMENT ITEM	1 SD	2 D	3 N	4 A	5 SA
1. We have incorporated cultural differences in our team processes.					
2. Our team is aware of different cultural ways of communicating, leading, and working together.					
3. We manage the challenge of geographic distances and time differences.					
4. Isolation and lack of social interactions are recognized.					
5. Control and coordination are balanced.					
6. Our team works collaboratively.					
7. Our team recognizes the importance of verbal and nonverbal communications.					
8. We are aware of the rich array of technological communication channels.					
9. We have developed and maintained teamness.					
10. Teams members trust one another.					

Scoring Key

45–50: Your team has successfully overcome the challenges of global work. You are able to work collaboratively together and produce strong results for your organization.

36–44: Your team is on the right track. You have the ability to be very successful. Examine where the difficulties lie (where your scores are lower). Have your team discuss strategies for addressing these issues. Reassess your team in three or four months to examine how you have addressed your concerns.

WORKSHEET 1 CONT'D

Assessing Challenges in Establishing and Maintaining Global Teams

25–35: Your team has met some of the challenges, but there are broad areas for improvement. Examine both your strengths and weaknesses. Examine ways you can learn from your strengths and apply them to your weaknesses.

24 or below: Your team has some challenges ahead. Review your score and choose one or two areas to concentrate your efforts. Taking on too much too soon may derail your team. As you meet with success, try transferring your learning to other areas.

Part Two

BRIDGES
AND
BOUNDARIES

Chapter 3

Effective Leadership

Teamwork and leadership often appear antithetical to one another. But as most of us have experienced and as research confirms, teamwork and leadership must not only coexist in high-performing teams—these two dynamics need each other for success. Teams that operate without strong leadership and good teamwork are unclear, unfocused, and without direction (Zaccaro and Marks, 1999).

When teams operate across cultural and geographic boundaries, leadership becomes even more critical to team success. According to leaders of successful global teams, their responsibilities require many more hours of work than they've ever devoted to co-located teams. Why? First, there are the complicated logistics. Then there's the greater need for thorough, timely documentation of everything—supported by graphs, charts, and other visuals to aid communication across language and culture barriers. Perhaps most significantly, there are the hours devoted to becoming personally acquainted with the team's members, learning about their national and organizational cultures, and dealing proactively with their diverse and sometimes clashing expectations regarding accountability, conflict, authority, decision making, feedback, deadlines, and more.

Although many of the factors that make for success in domestic work teams apply to global teams, the global environment introduces more variables and greater complexity. In their traditional roles of setting direction, making linkages, and managing team operations, global leaders must be able to handle a range of cultural behavior and expectations (responding to different leadership and followership styles, for example) and overcome the logistical challenges of working in different time zones and different locations with people of different professional backgrounds and unique operating customs and methods.

GUIDELINES FOR EFFECTIVE GLOBAL TEAM LEADERS

Each team is different. As a result, there are no tailor-made leadership strategies or a single model for the ideal global team leader. There are, however, some guidelines and general prescriptions for being effective in the various roles of a global team leader. In this chapter we examine five aspects of leadership in global teams:

- Leadership roles and processes that are necessary for high performance in teams
- How the global team environment influences the enactment of leadership roles
- Specific knowledge and skills that are necessary for global team leadership
- Qualities that are necessary for a global team leader's role
- Best practices for global team leaders

We will illustrate these aspects by examining a successful global team in the pharmaceutical industry: Glaxo-Wellcome. We have chosen the pharmaceutical industry because it is undergoing unprecedented levels of change. At the same time, current approaches to drug development are being actively challenged. Many pharmaceutical companies have responded to these changes in their industry by creating multifunctional global teams to discover, develop, and commercialize their portfolios of drug compounds. Their aim is to harness the best scientific talent irrespective of location, to maximize economies of scale throughout their value chain, and to ensure that the product reaches the widest population of consumers. What's more, pharmaceutical companies are examining every aspect of the way they do business—and global teams have been created to explore innovative solutions to present-day ways of working.

LEADERSHIP IN GLOBAL TEAMS AT GLAXO-WELLCOME

Karen Ward

Glaxo-Wellcome (GW), with 4.5 percent share of the global pharmaceutical market, is one of the leading health care companies. It is headquartered in the UK, has operating companies in seventy-six countries, and supplies over 150 markets globally. In 1999, it employed over 55,000 employees. GW describes itself as "research-based company whose people are committed to fighting disease by bringing innovative medicines and services to patients throughout the world and to the healthcare providers who serve them."

A global team was set up in the R&D part of the organization to ensure that GW Clinical Research "effectively and efficiently manages customer relationships at the investigator sites to create competitive advantage." There were signs that although Glaxo-Wellcome's relationships with its investigators were among the best in the industry, they were not optimal. The team was given the task of understanding customers' perception of their relationship with GW, exploring the causes of any dissatisfaction, and making recommendations for solutions.

The team sponsors, who are senior managers, represent key stakeholders across the company. They were appointed in late 1998. They then set about the task of appointing the team leader in early 1999. The successful candidate was female, British, and had a medical and commercial background. She had worked in the headquarters environment as well as one of the regional sales organizations, which made her appointment acceptable to two key stakeholders. She was appointed on the basis of her leadership and project skills, not because she was a technical expert in customer relations. This was an important departure from the norm in the pharmaceutical industry, where team leaders are often selected for their technical expertise despite evidence that this does not optimize team effectiveness.

Although the team leader was experienced in leading teams and projects, she had not led an international team before. She therefore requested that the facilitator who would work with the team had international teams as a core competence. One of the facilitator's key responsibilities was to coach the team leader and develop her awareness of the additional complexities of leading a culturally diverse team.

During the first few months of 1999, the team leader appointed the rest of the team. One of the key criteria was that the team's composition should reflect the wider organization both functionally and geographically. In the past, "international" teams had been set up to look for solutions to a variety of global problems and then had been staffed entirely from headquarters—with disastrous consequences when they tried to implement their "global" solution.

The team leader was unable to select all the team members personally, as the organization's culture enabled senior managers to nominate candidates to represent their part of the business. Although senior managers were given guidelines about the skills required to be an effective international team member, the team leader was not able to validate some of the selections until members had already joined the team.

The team that began the project had representatives from the key functions and from headquarters and local operating companies. But it also had people whose core job was interfacing with the very customers they were to study on this project. Geographically they represented England, Scotland, Sweden, Norway, Denmark, Australia, Canada, France, and both the east and west coasts of North America. Although the team did not cover the entire globe, it was a good representation of key markets. The team is now about halfway through its assignment and is on track to deliver a successful outcome—thanks to how they have developed and maintained shared leadership.

LEADERSHIP ROLES

Leadership is necessary in all types of team settings, including self-managed groups. Even in the absence of an official team leader, team members have to rely on leadership behavior from within the team and seek guidance from each other in order to provide focus and direction. The old style of leadership—driving employees to perform—must be replaced with motivating all members to create a common goal that drives them from within.

EFFECTIVE LEADERSHIP

How the leader carries out a role depends on the type of team he or she is leading. Teams vary by mission, composition, and level of the organization to which they belong. This is why there is no single prototype of good leadership behavior for teams. Effective leaders respond to the needs and environment of the particular team.

Within teams, leaders are called upon to use a broad range of leadership strategies and techniques—such as building consensus, using persuasion, and clarifying goals. To implement these strategies and techniques, leaders are called upon to perform four key roles: managing the team's external linkages; providing direction for team strategy and action; managing team operations (work processes); and acquiring adequate resources and organizational support. Through these four roles, the leader performs a number of important functions vital to team effectiveness. Let's examine each of them.

Managing External Linkages

While teams build boundaries around themselves to provide a sense of identity and purpose, the leader's job is to be aware of developments outside the team boundary that affect the team's mission and operations. With this information, the leader keeps the team aligned with the organization's strategy and operations. This involves linking with sources both inside and outside the team. The leader can learn, for example, how the organization views the team's performance and what resources are available. Learning what other teams are doing also provides information for aligning the team's task with the overall organizational goals.

Managing external linkages is a sequential process: first networking, then sense making, and then representing. Networking involves the development and maintenance of information sources inside and outside the team. These sources allow a team to gain the information they need to meet the expectations of external constituencies. Sense making involves creating meaning of the information gathered so it is helpful to the team. This includes understanding the forces, events, and dynamics that influence the evolving performance expectations of a team. Team representation involves representing the team to the outside world, safeguarding its interests, and shaping the environment to maximize support for the team (Zaccaro and Marks, 1999).

Setting Direction

As the team is forged, the leader turns to guiding the team toward self-management and setting its own direction. The manner in which the leader accomplishes these functions has a great influence on team effectiveness. In direction setting, for example, the leader who instills the belief that the team's goals are achievable contributes greatly to the likelihood of team success.

From the information developed as team liaison, the leader helps the team develop direction. This does not mean that the leader is just a funnel for transferring top management's objectives to the team. Strong leaders develop their own vision for the team and use their knowledge of what is going on outside the team to implement it. This includes accepting change in the outside world and adjusting the alignment of the team with the environment. In this light, the team vision, stimulated by the leader's direction, is aligned with that of the organization. When this alignment occurs, it gives team members motivation for success because they are more likely to perform well if they know that the team's output will have acceptance in the larger organization.

Setting a team's direction has two aspects. First, it means setting a clear and engaging vision with the details left unspecified. This communicates to a team what is important but allows them some means of providing input through specifying details (Hackman and Walton, 1986). Second, it means assisting a team in translating this vision into long-term strategies, short-term operational tactics, and then goals, plans, and tasks (Zaccaro and Marks, 1999).

Managing Team Operations

This role depends on the leader carrying out the other two roles of leadership—external linking and direction setting. After the team's direction is set, the leader helps the team to implement its strategies and goals through such activities as identifying needs, developing options for solutions, and selecting the best solution within the constraints of available resources. Global leaders can accomplish each of these roles in a number of basic ways. In the initial stages they recruit (or help select), develop, and motivate team members. At the same time they assess the team's needs.

Managing team operations includes developing and maintaining a group structure that promotes competent work on a task. This involves three elements: (1) developing a task that is motivating; (2) building a well-composed team in which members have task-relevant knowledge and skills; and (3) establishing clear norms of conduct specifying what must always be done and what can never be done.

Acquiring Adequate Resources and Organizational Support

A team must have adequate money, space, staff, time, and tools. Without these basic resources, a team will not be able to do its job. A leader must be able to provide a *reward system* that provides positive consequences for good performance, an *educational system* that provides the training and assistance a team may need, an *information system* that provides the data and projections needed for planning, and *sufficient material resources* that give the team the wherewithal to perform well (Hackman and Walton, 1986).

To accomplish any of these four roles, a leader will be engaged in two critical processes: monitoring and taking action. *Monitoring* is the gathering and interpretation of data about performance conditions and the events that affect them. This includes diagnosis—assessment of the current state of affairs—and projection about how things are changing and what events may occur. In *taking action*, the leader then needs to maintain a positive situation—exploiting opportunities and heading off problems—or improve a negative situation. These actions will either be inside the group or outside the group. Internal action is when the leader works with members to help them understand their tasks and processes. External action is when the leader works with the organization at large or with outside groups and individuals (McGrath, 1962; Hackman and Walton, 1986). Table 1 on the following page provides an overview of the four leadership functions with examples of the possible monitoring and action steps.

IMPACT OF CULTURAL DIFFERENCES

In fulfilling the four roles of team leadership, the global leader must be able to manage the cultural and organizational factors that differentiate

TABLE 1
Four Critical Leadership Functions and Processes

LEADERSHIP ROLES	EXAMPLES OF MONITORING AND ACTION
Managing external linkages • Networking • Sense making • Representing	• Gathering information from customers, clients, and peers • Developing a framework of the team's operating environment • Shaping the operating environment to maximize support for the team
Setting direction • Developing a clear, engaging vision • Helping the team translate that vision into long-term strategies, short-term operational tactics, and then goals, plans, and tasks	• Gathering information from team members concerning their understanding of the vision • Implementing team goals that are specific, measurable, and flexible
Managing team operations • Setting a motivating team task • Building a well-composed team • Establishing clear norms of conduct	• Revising the task structure so that members have a whole piece of meaningful work • Implementing a training program to help team members develop appropriate competencies • Establishing guidelines for what can and cannot be done
Acquiring adequate resources • Providing a reward system that provides positive consequences for good performance • Providing an educational system that provides training and assistance • Providing an information system that provides the data and projections needed for planning • Providing sufficient material resources	• Interviewing team members about their satisfaction with the current reward system • Implementing a training program to help team members develop interpersonal competencies • Examining future task information needs and the adequacy of the current system • Requesting additional staff from management given the new complexities of a task

a global team from a national team. In cross-cultural teams, for example, leaders may have to consider how they can maintain team cohesion over great distances and perhaps less frequent face-to-face meetings—in addition to being sensitive to cultural norms surrounding effective group behavior. Rather than considering the problems of leadership separately, the effect of these influences is better understood in the context of the four basic roles of team leadership. As we shall see, cultural factors impinge on each of these essential roles.

Culture and Managing External Linkages

The external linkage role involves recognizing developments outside the group that may affect the team's outcomes or processes. In the role of liaison, global team leaders are advocates for their teams and bridge the gaps between the team and the organization at large.

To give an example that illustrates the particular importance of the liaison function in global teamwork, it's useful to consider the impact of technology on team communications. Because the team relies on the organization for access to various communications media, the leader ensures that team members have the use of preferred technologies to support their different communication requirements according to the times and places they will be working (Devereaux and Johansen, 1994). As another example, global team leaders link the team with the performance expectations of its sponsors and stakeholders (Davison and Ward, 1999; Zaccaro and Marks, 1999). Global team leaders need to remember that responsiveness to the interests of local units is just as important as it is to the higher echelons of the organization.

In a global team the geographic spread of its members can influence a leader's ability to act as a liaison. The leader must find a way of keeping sponsors and team managers informed about the team's progress and problems. The best way to manage this is through two processes:

- Involve team members in different advocacy roles for the team by taking them to meetings and including them and acknowledging them in reports.

- Develop short summaries to update team sponsors and stakeholders on progress, or use shared databases and home pages on the web (Davison and Ward, 1999).

MANAGING COMMUNICATION AT GLAXO-WELLCOME

With the global team at Glaxo-Wellcome, the communication plan included a comprehensive review of group scope and objectives, a stakeholder map categorized by communication needs, an annual overview plan for the project, a communication matrix by groups, a list of the roles and responsibilities for communication, and an assessment of learning from communication. To ensure clarity of communication, a matrix was developed for all members of the project team to use.

Audience	Key Messages	Why	When	How	Feedback
Steering Group Committee	Initiation	Project approval	Feb.	Presentation and project definition document	From meeting
	Project Definition Document (plans and resource)	Gain approval of plans. Gain assistance in procuring resource.	March	E-mail 1:1 meetings	E-mail 1:1 meetings
	Steering Group Meeting	Issue resolution. Progress reporting. Plans. Escalate issues.	April	Written report via e-mail	E-mail 1:1 telephone

The work of the project was communicated widely throughout Glaxo-Wellcome in order to gain organizational endorsement. To accomplish this objective, a project definition was written and discussions were held with over 400 stakeholders. Both a two-page summary and a presentation package were developed for handouts. Poster sessions were presented at directors' meetings, and articles appeared in company newsletters. A web site was set up as a repository for all communications. In addition, customers were informed of the project's objectives.

EFFECTIVE LEADERSHIP

Culture and Setting Direction

A key component is keeping the team focused on its strategy and the attainment of goals through directing the team toward finding appropriate solutions (Zaccaro and Marks, 1999). To solve problems in a way that relates to the team's sense of what it needs, intuitive skills are also necessary. Global context influences a leader's ability to set a clear and engaging direction for the team. Three such influences are different cultural norms within the group, different levels of common language fluency, and culturally different leadership styles.

Differences in cultural norms are expressed through language, cognitive preferences, values, beliefs, status, artifacts, behavior, occupations, and functions. Whether visible or invisible, these norms will influence what members think are suitable goals for a team and what type of leadership they are comfortable with.

Although most global teams use a common language, there is a spectrum of fluency in global team settings. Differences in fluency can influence a person's ability to understand a conversation. What's more, these common languages have different norms for interrupting or gaining entry into a conversation. Sometimes non-native speakers may be totally excluded from a conversation (Davison, 1996). And, as we noted in Chapter 2, there are no universal expectations or norms for team leaders. Cultures differ drastically on how they expect a leader to direct interactions and take final action.

Because of these highly differing norms and expectations, the leader must set a clear direction in managing group perceptions in the early stages of the team's life. Either in the start-up phase or during the first meeting, a global team leader should engage in the following activities:

- Clarify in detail the team's mission, agenda, accountability, time frame, available resources, and key stakeholders. Using a group brainstorming and prioritizing technique that lets everyone contribute—and makes their contributions visual—can prevent anyone in the group from becoming dominant (and prevent anyone from being excluded).

- Interview the team players to get their understanding of the task, their perceptions of each other, and their commitment to the task. During the first meeting, make sure everyone is on board with the task process.

- Work through identifying, prioritizing, and agreeing to the purpose, objectives, and criteria for success.
- Work face-to-face in the early stages to build a working relationship (Davison, 1996).

SETTING DIRECTION AT GLAXO-WELLCOME

A clear purpose was created for this Glaxo-Wellcome team—namely, to "ensure that Glaxo-Wellcome Clinical Research effectively and efficiently manages customer relationships at the investigator site to create competitive advantage." The objectives developed were based on (1) an understanding of how we currently manage our customers at the investigator site, (2) where and why GW needs to change, (3) defining the stakeholders, the vision, changes, and business benefits, (4) defining the scope of the proposed program and its components, and (5) setting up measures for project/program success in a specific time frame.

Each meeting had defined objectives and outcomes. An example of one such meeting might be as follows:

KEY OBJECTIVE
- Learn who we are and why we are here
- Gain an understanding of the project, the methodology, and the approach
- Discuss initial fears and expectations

OUTCOME
- Know each other
- Understand overview of project plans, phases, workstreams, and methodology
- Understand expectations and fears
- Understand challenges of the project

AGENDA
- Activities to achieve all of the above

Cultural preferences were assessed to gain an understanding of the members' expectations of the group: (1) whether the leader should make the final decision or whether decisions are best made with the whole group;

(2) whether authority derives from one's position or is earned through one's achievements; (3) whether one should only say things that are relevant and well considered or should say whatever comes to mind; (4) whether one should distinguish clearly between private life and work life; and (5) whether high performance is reached by focusing on one thing at a time or by working at many things at once.

Culture and Managing Team Operations

Team management obviously involves a whole range of interpersonal actions and group dynamics. These come into play as the leader engages in a number of team-building functions: building confidence in the team's ability to achieve team goals, motivating team members to undertake problem solving, creating common understandings, and assisting team members individually. Two aspects have a particular impact on the leader's ability to manage a global team: different expectations of effective group behavior and different expectations of leadership (Davison and Ward, 1999).

Effective team management requires extra effort in learning the team members' expectations and styles of operating. Assessing the members' potential, the leader needs cultural sensitivity in order to recognize strengths and weaknesses without cultural bias. Here cultural factors become extremely important. Not all of them can be known in advance. To avoid having the team's functioning brought to a halt, it may be necessary to bring in expert intercultural facilitators. Regardless of how open team members may be to cultural diversity, working in a cross-cultural environment is deeply fatiguing (Devereaux and Johansen, 1994).

To overcome language barriers, misunderstandings, and different values calls for concentrated effort as well. The global team leader needs to be sensitive to these extra efforts required of team members—making decisions about how long and how frequent meetings should be, for example, or how to keep up morale and willingness to work when progress is slow, especially in the early phases of the team's life.

Another area of team leadership complicated by global team functioning is the distribution of resources, which includes managing the flow of information. Leadership that does not plan for the processing of information quickly falls into trouble. Incorrect or outdated information can cause significant misunderstandings and weaken the team. This is particularly true on global teams, where different cultures value different presentation styles. Leaders can help forge compromise or dual modes of communication that satisfy the needs of all members to be adequately informed without overload (Devereaux and Johansen, 1994).

In fact, the challenge of cultural diversity can be a plus—if, and this is crucial, the team leaders utilize this potential. Global HR managers point out that a major value of service on global teams is that it provides cross-pollination. Team members can be guided to see the strengths of each culture and note how cultural synergies can generate more creativity for the organization as a whole (Marmer, 1995).

Importance of Leadership During the Early Stages

The leader's informed skill is rarely more critical than during the first weeks of the team's formation. Before the first meeting, the leader must hammer out the team's purpose with its executive sponsors and then gauge the members' aggregate strengths and weaknesses. (This information should be shared with team members so that ways of compensating for weaknesses can be devised.) Worthwhile, too, is trying to persuade local managers to include an employee's performance on the global team in personnel evaluations.

The team's first meeting paves the way for long-term success. For example, a leader we respect held the first meeting at a site unfamiliar to all (including himself) and focused on discovering commonalities among the members, not on dissecting their differences. With customer service as the topic of discussion, all members had equal time to share insights they had gained working back home. And all cited ideas that were cross-nationally transferable. The leader was careful to model respect for each team member by listening carefully, asking clarifying questions, and neither interrupting nor permitting interruptions. Finally, he ensured that there was free time for all simply to have fun together.

The global team leader can actively engage in some activities at the first meeting to deal with different expectations of leadership and group process. These activities include:

- Establishing an understanding of the team's composition that emphasizes complementary skills and knowledge

- Contracting with an external facilitator to guide group process (see Chapter 9)

- Suggesting face-to-face meetings and social gatherings to build working relationships

- Having the team engage in a guided discussion to examine its strengths and weaknesses based on cultural differences

- Helping the team agree on the first set of tasks and who will be doing what, when, and how

- Checking to see that everyone is involved and using the method of feedback that was agreed upon

Management on global teams involves influencing team members. It also means paying careful attention to team input in establishing a team identity, setting realistic objectives, and creating a supportive work environment. Validating what members have to say and acknowledging their contributions is especially important when, for example, team members from local units feel they have less status than representatives from headquarters. One task of the leader in a culturally diverse team is to create a team vision that inspires all members to do more than what they thought possible (Davison and Ward, 1999).

ASSESSING TEAM MEMBERS' SATISFACTION AT GLAXO-WELLCOME

At regular intervals, the following questions were posed to all Glaxo-Wellcome team members. The responses were collected (using a Likert scale ranging from "fully agree" to "completely disagree") and then discussed:

- I fully understand the requirements of this project.
- I feel my contributions are listened to by my colleagues.
- I have been able to contribute to the discussions as much as I want.
- I know what I need to do for this project in the next three months.
- I am confident I can manage the key stakeholders for this project.
- I am happy with the way we are working together.
- I am clear what I need to deliver for this project to be successful.

- I am able to use my skills and expertise fully within this team.
- I am valued by my colleagues.
- I am enjoying being on this team.

Culture and Acquiring Adequate Resources and Organizational Support

Global leaders need to be sure that their team has adequate resources. The most difficult aspect of resourcing global teams is that members usually come from cross-functional boundaries. This means that the global manager will often have to work with many line managers to find the needed human and financial resources within the desired time frame. Thus a global team leader must have frequent contact and negotiations on resource issues with line managers. Before the team meets for the first time, it is also important for the leader to assess members' competencies for the task through informal interviews and to develop the opportunities for training where appropriate. Table 2 summarizes the major roles of the global team leader, the influence of global environment on the functional role, and the strategies for dealing with it.

ESSENTIAL KNOWLEDGE AND SKILLS

Like any other team leader, the global leader will need skills for *monitoring* (data-gathering skills, diagnostic skills, forecasting skills) and skills for *taking action* (envisioning skills, negotiation skills, decision-making skills). To assess a team's present status and predict its future needs, the team leader must be able to collect data, develop inferences, test hypotheses, and improve social systems. Leaders can develop these skills through:

- Participating in programs on data collection, research method management systems, communication, negotiation, and decision making
- Engaging in a diagnostic project within the company with the help of an organizational development expert
- Examining case studies of teams in the academic and trade literature

EFFECTIVE LEADERSHIP

TABLE 2
Global Context and Team Functions

TEAM LEADER'S FUNCTION	INFLUENCE OF GLOBAL CONTEXT	TEAM LEADER'S STRATEGY
Managing external linkages • Networking • Sense making • Representing	• Geographic spread (e.g., different time zones) and different locations (e.g., headquarters and field offices) of team members	• Involve team members in different advocacy roles by taking them to meetings and acknowledging them in reports
Setting direction • Developing a clear, engaging vision • Helping the team translate that vision into strategies, short-term operational tactics, and then goals, plans, and tasks	• Different cultural norms within the group • Different levels of language fluency • Culturally different leadership styles	• Clarify the team's purpose, agenda, accountability, time frame, available resources, and key stakeholders using a group brainstorming and prioritizing technique
Managing team operations • Setting a motivating team task • Building a well-composed team • Establishing clear norms of conduct	• Different expectations of effective group behavior • Different expectations of leadership	• Help members understand the team's composition by emphasizing complementary skills and knowledge
Acquiring adequate resources • Providing a reward system that provides positive consequences for good performance • Providing an educational system that provides training and assistance • Providing an information system that provides the data and projections needed for planning • Providing sufficient material resources	• Members' cross-functional boundaries	• Assess members' competencies for the task through informal interviews, and develop opportunities for training

To help the group take action and perform at a higher level, the leader must develop skills in creativity, communicating, convincing others, making decisions in uncertain situations, helping others to learn, and getting things done. Hackman and Walton's (1986) comprehensive list of these diagnostic, forecasting, and action skills is shown in Table 3.

The global context puts the leader in a role of motivating people from a wide variety of regions and time zones. This entails a knowledge of cultural norms, the ability to manage through different technologies, and the skill to communicate in the language of choice. In most global teams, members have different native tongues but choose one language to work in. Thus global team leaders do not have to speak several languages, but they must work easily in the business language. Each of these competencies is discussed here:

Cultural knowledge: understanding the cultural dimension of nationalities and their implications. This refers to Geert Hofstede's (1991) and Fons Trompenaars' (1994) work on the dimensions of culture—issues explored in greater depth in Chapter 6. This knowledge allows a leader to understand the behavior of global team members in the cultural context and to adopt a style that is more acceptable from a broad section of nationalities (Davison and Ward, 1999).

Language skills: the ability to converse coherently in the business language of the team.

Communication flexibility: the ability to communicate, manage, motivate, and influence via a wide variety of communication tools (e-mail, phone, videoconferencing).

Table 4 presents these cross-cultural competencies. Training activities—including job experiences and developmental relationships—can help improve any of these cross-cultural skills. Such activities include:

- Participating in classes (either internal or external) on cross-cultural management and communication technology

- Working with a coach who observes your interactions in a cross-cultural context and provides specific feedback

- Engaging in cross-cultural assignments in which you are working and communicating in different cultures

TABLE 3
Diagnostic, Forecasting, and Action Skills for Team Leaders

SKILL	DESCRIPTION	TYPE
Data-gathering skill	Ability to collect data about social systems that are reliable and valid (the data mean what they appear to mean)	Diagnostic/forecasting
Diagnostic and forecasting skill	Ability to apprehend complexity and make sense of it, drawing on both data and current knowledge in shaping conclusions	Diagnostic/forecasting
Hypothesis-testing skill	Ability to use data to assess relative validity of alternative hypotheses about the state of a social system (or forecasting its likely future state)	Diagnostic/forecasting
Learning skill	Ability to learn about leadership and management and apply what is learned in understanding social systems and planning action to change them	Diagnostic/forecasting
Envisioning skill	Ability to envision desired end states and then communicate them to others	Taking action
Inventive skill	Ability to think of numerous ways of getting something done	Taking action
Negotiation skill	Ability to work persistently and constructively with peers and superiors to secure the resources or assistance needed to support subordinates	Taking action
Decision-making skill	Ability to choose among various courses of action, despite uncertainty, using all perspectives and data that can be efficiently obtained to inform the decision	Taking action
Teaching skill	Ability to help others learn both experientially and didactically	Taking action

TABLE 3 (CONTINUED)
Diagnostic, Forecasting, and Action Skills for Team Leaders

SKILL	DESCRIPTION	TYPE
Interpersonal skill	Ability to communicate, listen, confront, persuade—generally to work constructively with other people, particularly when anxieties may be high	Taking action
Implementation skill	Ability to get things done—at a simple level, knowing how to make lists, attend to mundane details, check and recheck for omitted items or people, and follow plans through to completion; at a more sophisticated level, being able to constructively and assertively manage power, political relationships, and symbols to get things accomplished in social systems	Taking action

Source: Adapted from Hackman and Walton (1986).

TABLE 4
Cross-Cultural Skills/Knowledge

SKILL	DESCRIPTION	TYPE
Knowledge of cultural norms	Understanding the cultural dimension of nationalities and their implications	Cross-cultural communication
Language skills	Knowing how to speak and understand the business language of the team	Cross-cultural communication
Communication flexibility	Knowing how to communicate, manage, motivate, and influence using a wide variety of communication tools (e-mail, phone, videoconferencing)	Cross-cultural communication

EFFECTIVE LEADERSHIP

ATTRIBUTES OF SUCCESSFUL GLOBAL TEAM LEADERS

Not everyone can be a global team leader. This complicated role involves managing learning, global interactions, and team dynamics. Not everyone possesses the skills and competencies to engage in this type of complexity. In fact, there's evidence that there are certain team leadership traits. Although a host of qualities are listed—including creativity, systematic thinking, and emotional values—three traits are essential if a leader is to work with a global team effectively: courage, openness, and empathy.

Courage requires the global team leader to be willing to buck the tide and create the necessary conditions for effectiveness whatever the obstacles. Leaders must be able to risk angering members in order to establish effective team process. Here are some managerial practices that promote courage:

- Challenging group norms
- Disrupting established routines in the team and the organization
- Risking incurring the displeasure of peers and superiors in order to assist the team with resources

Openness requires that global leaders be willing to suspend their need for control as well as possess "cultural humility." To process multiple levels of experience, they must be able to see their own values, background, and experiences as neither better nor worse than the values, background, and experiences of others. Here are some managerial practices that promote openness:

- Commitment to cultural diversity and selection, development, and promotion
- Conflict resolution skills
- Ready availability of all information to all members

Empathy allows global team leaders to be sensitive to human nature and be capable of repairing strained relationships. Here are some managerial practices that are socially responsible and respectful of individual dignity:

- Strong sense of ethics in dealing with employees, customers, clients
- Active corporate citizenship
- Recognition of employees' contributions outside the workplace
- Willingness to take responsibility for relationships

Leaders without empathy, courage, and openness will find they have trouble expressing consistency in their behavior, taking action on essential team business, and navigating the turbulent waters of cross-cultural expectations and behavioral expressions.

BEST PRACTICES

To develop leadership for global teams, organizations need to recognize both the general qualities that contribute to leadership in a group and the special factors that characterize leadership in cross-national and cross-cultural teams. The following guidelines provide a path that—if adapted to the mission, the team's composition, and its geographic extent—will lead to development of those leadership qualities necessary for high performance in global teams. Global leaders should:

- Succeed in the four roles of team leadership: managing the team's external links, providing direction for team strategy and action, managing team operations (work processes), and acquiring adequate resources throughout the life of the team
- Possess monitoring, action, and cross-cultural competencies
- Demonstrate qualities of openness, systemic thinking, creativity, personal efficacy, and empathy

STRONG LEADERSHIP OF GLOBAL TEAMS

To be an effective leader of a global team demands almost superhuman skills. Among other attributes, one must be flexible, be willing to support the team process, help the team work together, understand team cultural factors, be able to listen and communicate, and be able to understand other members' behavior (Marmer, 1995).

Although being a leader of a global team may not require you to be a superman or superwoman, it does, as Davison and Ward (1999) point out, require "attention to such a complexity of factors that an individual will invariably not be able to attend to all of them" (p. 178). As we saw in the Glaxo-Wellcome case, global teams need competent and confident leaders to navigate the immense challenges of the global environment. In Chapter 4 we show how developing a clear vision is essential for global leaders and team success.

Chapter 4

Creating a Vision and Team Identity

When people enter a team they are usually struck with two significant questions: "Why are we here?" and "Why am I part of this team?" Providing a clear, challenging team vision and building a shared, compelling team identity can help team members to answer these questions and thus bring much-needed power to global teams. The goal of this chapter is to explore the process and consequences of creating a vision for a global team. We'll survey three specific topics: a global team's need for a vision; the process of developing a global team vision; and the relationship of a vision to creating a team identity.

NEED FOR A COMPELLING VISION

A team's vision gives its members "stars to steer by." A powerful vision guides and inspires, motivates and excites, and ultimately gives meaning and importance to the activities of people both inside and outside the team. It gives team members a sense of who they are and what they stand for. A highly effective team vision also allows a team to connect to the broader organization.

Try to think of an organization that has achieved and sustained some measure of greatness without a vision. You probably can't. Taco Bell's vision was to "become number one in the stomach"; Federal Express delivers packages "absolutely, positively overnight"; Polaroid provides "instant photography." Each of these organizations was able to bind people together around a common identity and sense of destiny. So too should a global team develop a powerful purpose and vision.

A vision can capture the team's hopes, goals, and direction for the future. It will become the image of the team that is transmitted inside and outside the organization. Jim Gannon, vice-president of human resource planning and development for Royal Bank of Canada, underscores the decisive importance of a vision for global teams when he says that "visions are what energize teams; they represent the dreams that pull us forward" (Marquardt, 1999).

A team vision should include a clear statement of purpose as well as a mission statement. The vision is the essential element that allows members to work toward a common goal rather than at cross-purposes. A clear vision can prevent the all-too-common hazard of each member developing his or her personal idea of what the team should be doing— or, worse still, working against the goals of the organization (Smolek et al., 1999).

The purpose and direction conveyed by a vision contribute positively to effective collaboration, commitment, and productivity in a team setting (Niehoff et al., 1990; Tjosvold and Tsao, 1989). A vision helps a team to align with the goals of an organization, clarify its members' roles, and inspire action. By setting a direction, a team can focus its energy and activities. The vision can assure others that the team is performing within the boundaries and expectations of its stakeholders (Zaccaro and Marks, 1999).

Unfortunately, not all team visions are effective, clear, exciting, significant, or meaningful to employees and other stakeholders. Without these characteristics, however, the vision can easily dissolve into a list of confusing and incompatible projects that can take the team in the wrong direction or nowhere at all. Kotter (1996) cites a useful rule of thumb: If you can't communicate the team's vision to someone in five minutes or less and get a reaction that signifies both understanding and interest, you are not yet finished with this phase of building the global team.

In seeking to become a global team, the vision should depict the ideal team of the future in which:

- There are no geographic barriers to opportunities

CREATING A VISION AND TEAM IDENTITY

- The entire world is the marketplace for members, partners, and resources
- Multiple cultures are present and synergized
- Achieving the team's mission and goals requires global thinking and action

Why is a vision of "globalness" so important for becoming a global team? First: A vision provides the focus and energy for overcoming the established corporate culture that promotes a "local-is-best" mentality. A global vision encourages people to switch from a nationalistic to a global perspective.

Second: The loftiness of a global target compels new ways of thinking and acting. It provides a rudder to keep the global team on course when pressure builds to return to local ways of doing things.

Third: Powerful commitment to difficult goals only occurs when people are truly committed to accomplishing things that matter deeply to them. The shared vision and values of globalness allow people to change, to accept new ways of thinking, to give up deeply held views that are no longer productive.

It's important to remember that people are not machines but individuals who live within various cultures. They need a collective sense of identity and fundamental purpose for living their lives. Visions should be exhilarating. They should create the spark and excitement that enable the organization to develop renowned products and services. Through a shared vision, global teams can shape the direction as well as develop the structures, activities, and people necessary to achieve success. The global vision should guide strategic thinking and planning for the team as well as determine the values and norms that will guide its work.

WHO DEVELOPS THE GLOBAL TEAM'S VISION?

A vision is not always readily apparent. In most organizational contexts the multitude of trends and forces in the immediate environment suggest many different directions for a team to take. Given that no two stakeholders have the same relationship with the collective team, these directions are usually contradictory. The team's leader, with the help of its members, must decide its direction given its purpose, resources, and capabilities. Thus a successful vision must align with the trends and expectations of the organization and the changing environment (Zaccaro and Marks, 1999).

Of course, team leaders must take part in developing the team's vision. As Charles Handy (1995, p. 1) notes: "A leader shapes and shares a vision which gives point to the work of others." This does not mean, however, that the team leader develops the vision without consulting others. The team leader creates a working vision. To create buy-in and support, the leader must encourage all team members to modify and shape the direction that has been set.

VISIONS FOR GLOBAL TEAMS AT PFIZER

At Pfizer the vision of the global teams is based on three factors:

- The vision/goal must be a business or performance challenge that is best addressed by a global team.
- The global teams must stay focused on achieving goals that are directly tied to business results that align team members' accountability.
- Territorial or "silo" cultures should not be allowed to threaten the formation of team visions.

See Chapter 8 for an illustration of how Pfizer develops its global teams.

IMPLEMENTING A TEAM VISION

Visions in and of themselves are nebulous. For instance, a strategy team in a software organization may have a vision to "generate significant growth in our company through identifying and selecting markets, partnerships, and products." Such a vision provides little guidance to team members given the multiple meanings of the words used and the lack of clarity concerning implementation. "Significant growth," for instance, could have many different meanings for each team member. And the process of "identifying and selecting markets" can involve many different strategies (Zaccaro and Marks, 1999).

For a vision to be effective, it must be able to be translated into long-term team strategies and short-term operational tactics as well as specific goals, plans, and tasks. In essence, a team is a goal-seeking group. Thus the cornerstone of a successful vision is its operationalization into tasks that are specific and doable; Zaccaro and Marks, 1999).

Once the team's vision and purpose are developed, the group must identify the tasks that will help it achieve its overarching goals (Forsyth, 1999). Effective tasks for a team have nine characteristics: they must (1) be difficult, (2) be specific, (3) be linked to resources and capabilities, (4) be measurable, (5) provide a basis for team feedback and rewards, (6) generate commitment, (7) be flexible and adaptive, (8) coordinate vertically with other organizational goals, and (9) coordinate horizontally with other team and unit goals (Zaccaro and Marks, 1999).

GUIDELINES FOR CREATING A GLOBAL TEAM VISION

Visions serve several purposes. First, they force a team to evaluate its fundamental attributes and characteristics. Second, they set boundaries to guide future strategy—specifically by setting limits to what a team will engage in as well as what it won't. Finally, a vision sets standards of performance (Marquardt, 1996).

In examining successful global teams, we note a number of guidelines for designing and implementing a global team vision:

- Create a team charter and mission statement that reflects the team's vision so as to institutionalize the team's purpose and create a sense of team identity.

- Translate the vision into long-term strategies, short-term operational tactics, and then goals, plans, and tasks.

- Create the team vision through some sort of collaborative process with team members.

- Identify the team's key strategic focus (efficiency, local responsiveness, organizational learning), link it to the organization's strategic intent, and communicate this vision to team members.
- Depict the team's vision in key words and simple graphics that are universally understood and accepted.

To create and implement a successful team vision, two steps are necessary: Develop a charter, and prepare a mission statement.

DEVELOPING THE CHARTER

The charter, which is usually developed by management, establishes expectations through the definition of outcomes, goals, and measurement. Such graphic pictures of the vision clarify the roles, boundaries, and communication process (Smolek et al., 1999). Essential elements in a charter include:

Goals: The charter provides both task and process goals that are clear, specific, and measurable.

Expectations: The charter sets expectations (by team members and stakeholders) that are clear, specific, measurable, and aimed at high performance, and that address such issues as logistics (attendance, timeliness, notification, conduct, participation, role performance, preparation, task performance, and so forth).

Policies and procedures: The charter establishes policies that address key performance areas, are enforceable, and will help manage team performance.

Time line and project plan: The charter divides the project into tasks with an appropriate time line and completion dates; tasks are assigned to specific team members; specific process checks and checkpoints (such as a team consultant) are included.

Roles: Both task and process roles are clearly defined and assigned to specific team members; role assignments are explained.

Worksheet 2 presents a guide to help the organization and team members develop a charter for their global team.

WORKSHEET 2

Components and Procedures for Creating a Global Team Charter

Directions: This worksheet details the essential components for an effective global team charter. It is designed to help you collaborate with team members, set expectations, design preliminary performance management systems, and provide a mechanism for evaluating team members. As part of the charter, team members should develop a project plan detailing the team's goals, the members' roles, a time line, and project tasks.

GOALS

State your team's goals clearly and specifically. Be sure to emphasize the goals concerning the main work of the team and the goals concerning how the team will organize around the task.

EXPECTATIONS/MEASURABLE BEHAVIOR

Decide as a team on the categories of performance that members consider essential to the long-term success of the team. (As a rule of thumb, teams usually find that five or six expectations are manageable. More than that number is cumbersome, and fewer is inadequate. Expectations might include attendance at meetings, and meeting deadlines.) Describe the specific, measurable behavior that constitutes high performance in each of the categories. For example:

PARTICIPATION IN TELEPHONE CONFERENCES AND MEETINGS [CATEGORY]

- Each member shall participate in all meetings [specific behavior]

POLICIES

Your team should then decide on its policies. These define the boundaries of behavior for team members and specify when a person has not met a team's expectations and the corrective action that will be taken. For example:

- A team member's first missed work deadline will result in a verbal warning.

The team should also define the rewards that members will receive if they go the extra mile for the team. For example:

- If a team member performs a task in an exemplary fashion we will treat him or her to an ice cream.

WORKSHEET 2 CONT'D

Components and Procedures for Creating a Global Team Charter

PROCEDURES
The team defines how it will specifically enforce the polices and procedures developed. For example, in the procedure for issuing a reward:

- Prior to issuing a reward, the team will meet to discuss the exemplary behavior and vote on the reward.

TIME LINE AND PROJECT PLAN
The team assigns tasks to specific people with clear due dates. In this category four distinct steps are suggested:

- Divide the main goals into tasks.
- Assign each task to a team member.
- Develop a time line for the project, including completion dates.
- Define the process the team will use to evaluate a member's progress.

ROLES
In this final section of the charter, the team assigns permanent roles concerning the team's main work and how it will organize around this work. Two distinct steps are suggested:

- Define both the task and the process roles.
- Assign roles to team members.

PREPARING THE MISSION STATEMENT

The charter is not the end of the process for developing the team's vision. A charter is merely the launching point of creating a dialogue that will assist the team in developing its mission statement—in essence, the members' understanding of the team's essential purpose and vision. An effective mission statement must align with the organizational mission, fulfill the needs of the charter, and meet the expectations of various stakeholders such as customers, team members, and managers. The mission statement is, basically, the written vision (Smolek et al., 1999).

The effective mission statement has six elements: (1) an organization's basic purpose, (2) its distinctive characteristics, (3) how it will evolve in the long term, (4) its principal stakeholders, (5) its principal products or services, and (6) its basic beliefs, values, and aspirations. The dialogue starts with creating a vision and continues as the team establishes its operational goals and plans and defines needed resources (Smolek et al., 1999).

VALUES OF COLGATE-PALMOLIVE GLOBAL TEAMS

Colgate-Palmolive's vision as an organization is to "become the best truly global consumer products company." The entire organization and all global teams and their members are expected to practice the following corporate values:

- **Truly global:** We seek to bring together the world's best people, creative ideas, technology, and processes to meet the needs of our consumers wherever they live. We create and sustain superior business performance through global teams and global teamwork.

- **Continuous improvement:** We are committed to getting better every day in all we do—as individuals and in our teams. By better understanding consumers' expectations, and by always working to improve our products, services, and processes, we strive to become the best.

- **Caring:** We care about all Colgate people. This shared value means that each of us listens with respect, values differences, builds mutual trust, and supports our unity of purpose and action. We care also for the best interests of our consumers, shareholders, business partners, our many local communities, and the protection of the global environment.

- **Consumer focus:** We are committed to listening to consumers and responding to their needs and preferences. With this unwavering consumer focus, we will achieve our end goal: to deliver quality products and services that exceed consumers' expectations.

In the Colgate-Palmolive case described in Chapter 10, team members emphasize that the team's clear vision and its direct connection to the company's values and mission led to their numerous successes.

IDENTITY AS A BY-PRODUCT OF A TEAM VISION

Developing a shared sense of identity is often difficult in a global team environment—given that teams are often spread across geographical regions, time zones, and cultural regions. The boundaries of time, space, and culture often make the use of electronic communication such as e-mail, videoconferencing, and telephones the primary means of interaction in the team. These forms of electronic communication, however, do not allow for much in the way of developing symbols or transmitting information about group members (Ashforth and Mael, 1989; Dutton et al., 1994).

Group identity is basically the awareness and attraction of members to one another. This process is of concern because when members begin to identify with one another, the group's cohesiveness and performance increase (Hogg, 1996; Ashforth and Mael, 1989. The reduction of social information and the asynchronous nature of most computer-mediated communications, however, delay the development of identity in a global team. Thus the ability to form a sense of groupness is lost.

One way to develop a sense of team identity is to give the team a place and time to discuss itself—perhaps through the development of tangible representations such as a charter, a logo, slogans, or a mission statement. One critical by-product of the vision statement is the development of team identity and thus team cohesion and performance.

UNIQUE CHALLENGES

A shared vision, as we have seen, allows the team to create a unifying corporate culture in a context containing many distinct ethnic cultures. This team vision can celebrate the diversity and highlight the similarities in a global team. A team vision is the perfect place to display its accep-

CREATING A VISION AND TEAM IDENTITY

tance of diverse viewpoints by team members. As Devereaux and Johansen (1994, p. 234) point out: "A vision that truly reflects the wealth of the organization's human assets acts as a 'global glue' for operating units that often look quite different from one another."

When clarifying the global team's mission and purpose, all key stakeholders should be present—such as country/line managers—since they are the ones who need to work out their relationship to team members, change the HR support systems, and agree on budgeting issues (Davison and Ward, 1999).

As we noted in Chapter 1, global teams offer a number of distinct advantages to an organization. Three of the most important benefits are:

Global efficiency: reduced duplication, cutting the number and cost of suppliers, and creating products that are acceptable in many countries simultaneously

Local responsiveness: the extent to which products and advertising are sensitive to the local political, legal, and economic framework

Organizational learning: spreading innovation, transferring knowledge, and integrating a variety of interests (Bartlett and Ghoshal, 1998)

Each of these major benefits—and thus goals for the team—has different implications for implementation and management. When global efficiency is the goal, a team leader must pay attention to equality between team members. When the goal is local responsiveness, teams must be especially responsive to the less powerful and minority voices. And when the team focuses on organizational learning, the team will need support to navigate around organizational barriers (Davison and Ward, 1999).

Given that clarity of purpose and mission are factors in the success of any team—especially global teams—one must make a clear link between corporate global strategy and team purpose. Motivation and commitment are lost when the team's relation to the organization is left unclear (Davison and Ward, 1999). Therefore a team leader must identify the team's key strategic focus (efficiency, local responsiveness, organizational learning), link it to the organization's strategic intent, and then communicate it to team members.

DEVELOPING THE VISION FOR GMU'S
GLOBAL INTEGRATION TEAM

Chan Chee Keong, Asian Team Member

In 1997 General Motors created the GM University Global Integration Team for the purpose of globalizing programs worldwide. The GMU team was composed of four members: a Brazilian representing the Latin American region, a British person stationed in Zurich to represent Europe, a Singaporean for the Asia/Pacific region, and an American at GM headquarters in Detroit. The team began in October 1997. It continues to meet face-to-face every six months in Detroit and holds weekly telephone conference calls.

In developing its vision and objectives, the team faced several key questions:

- What are the training needs of the various regions?
- What are the common processes and training needs so that programs can be offered globally: leadership development at various management levels under the GMU umbrella, leadership competencies for high potential, and so forth?
- How can we avoid redundancy at regional and national levels?
- Can we create a modular curriculum?
- How do we tie in with the global manufacturing system?
- How can we coordinate the development of global curriculum with subject matter experts?
- How will we use technology, and how can we transfer it quickly?
- How can we create and reinforce global perspectives?
- How can we gain people's acceptance in the various regions?
- How can we maintain quality but keep costs low?

These questions have guided the team and, I believe, enable us to be very successful. Our mission and vision have become well defined, challenging, and motivating. Team members have very clear roles. They recognize that they are to fully represent regional interests as well as the worldwide interests of GM. We are a small, manageable group, all of whom are committed to achieving the team's vision. The high level of trust among members has fostered strong team cohesiveness. Finally, because our team's vision and mission match the goal of GMU, we have received organizational commitment and sufficient funding for supporting the team's global and regional vision.

BRIDGING THE VISION AND IDENTITY WITH TRUST

Devereaux and Johansen (1994) emphasize that sustaining team identity is very difficult in a global and predominantly electronic environment—unless team members feel they have a common vision and a common identity. Solid personal relationships must be built early in the life of the team. Otherwise, the cohesiveness created by the vision and identity may disintegrate under pressures of work and the demands of globally diverse colleagues. Building swift trust thus becomes a key ingredient of successful global teams—an ingredient we explore in Chapter 5.

Chapter 5

Building Swift Trust and Strong Norms

Here's a scenario all too familiar to members of a global organization. You have just been assigned to work on a project, one that has a short deadline and is vital to the company. If it's a success, you know it could have a very positive effect on your career. The scale of the project is too large for you to accomplish on your own, however, and the project involves varied competencies possessed only by people dispersed across your organization's international sites. Therefore employees from offices around the world have been assigned to this project.

The success of the project depends on each person coming through with the work they are assigned. You don't know these people, nor will you have time to meet them face-to-face. How can you rely on people you have never met—and will only meet through videoconferencing, telephone, and e-mail—to come through on this critical project? How can you trust that they will be productive, harmonious teammates? How can you create good communications and strong norms?

These are the questions we will pursue in this chapter. As we shall see, the building of swift trust is the glue that binds the global team together and keeps it together. It not only builds effective and efficient communications but helps to establish the norms that will guide the group across the boundaries of time, distance, and culture.

IMPORTANCE OF BUILDING SWIFT TRUST

Global teams do not usually have time to get to know each other well. Often they must focus quickly on critical tasks and have little time for building relationships or even for in-person contact. Yet the successful global team requires a high level of trust among its members. Trust is critical especially in organizational arrangements where teams are dispersed geographically (Jarvenpaa et al., 1998).

Simply defined, trust is the team members' reliance on one another to protect their joint endeavor. In every type of team, performance is always dependent on the level of trust established within the team. Trust is difficult to enforce in a team setting, however, since you can't compel team members to trust each other. Rather, trust must arise from people's willingness to cooperate and anticipate the benefits from their cooperation (Hosmer, 1995).

In global teams trust is even more difficult to achieve. It is asking a lot to expect people to protect the interests of their fellow team members—given that they may be total strangers with totally different ways of thinking and acting. Thus the building of trust and a team culture from a variety of national norms, values, and traditions is often an overwhelming task.

Even so, building swift trust is imperative for the success of a global team. Trust usually occurs as a direct result of demonstrated action over time—through a combination of mutual experience, bargaining, testing, and reflection. When a team spends time constructing, negotiating. and carrying out team goals, for example, it provides opportunities for members to learn about each other and thereby demonstrate their good faith and commitment to each other.

Within the global context, however, face-to-face relationships and the traditional opportunities to establish trust as the result of mutual experience are frequently absent. Members of global teams are usually located in different geographic areas and therefore do not have a chance to build trust in a gradual, cumulative fashion.

The challenge, then, is to create trust quickly within the global team. This is the concept of swift trust—when team members act as if trust is present from the beginning. Swift trust can be defined as the "willingness of an individual to be vulnerable to the actions of another party without the ability to control or monitor, and based on the expectation that the other person will perform" (Jarvenpaa et al., 1998).

BUILDING SWIFT TRUST ON MMD'S GLOBAL TRANSITION TEAM

Joe Bocchino, Global Team Member

Marion Merrell Dow (MMD) is a global pharmaceutical company with annual sales of approximately $3 billion that include products for heart disease, allergies, gastrointestinal disorders, antibiotics, mouthwash and lozenges, and smoking cessation products (such as Nicorette). In December 1989, MMD underwent a merger that brought together two very different companies:

- **Marion Company** (originally Marion Laboratories), based in Kansas City, had 99 percent of its manufacturing and sales in the United States. Until 1989 Marion had operated from its Kansas City headquarters in a very hierarchical, patriarchal, traditional manner with modest manufacturing technology and limited efficiency.

- **Merrell Dow Pharmaceuticals** (MDP), originally based in Cincinnati, was a global pharmaceutical company with one-third of its business coming from outside the United States. MDP included a composite of companies such as Merrell National Labs, Pitman Moore, Lakeside Pharmaceuticals, Lepetit (Italian), and Dow Pharmaceuticals.

As an immediate consequence of the merger, trust was low. Each company felt it must compete with its new partner to remain viable. In the years before the merger, many sites of both companies had been closed. As far as the Marion people were concerned, the Merrell Dow people were arrogant and reluctant to share ideas and technology. In both companies, key managers were fearful about job security.

To deal with these issues, an MMD global manufacturing technology team was established. Membership included a representative from eleven different sites in Asia, Europe, and North America plus two people from the global headquarters. Nationalities included Canadian, French, Italian, Brazilian, Pakistani, German, and American.

The thirteen team members recognized that they first needed to build a platform of mutual trust and understanding as a mechanism for bringing the group together. They initiated this process by developing a common vision in which they identified the desired goals and ideal state for the company, using a framework of two to three years. They also categorized the needs of each site as well as the company at large. Here are some examples of the needs for each site:

- **Kansas City:** With over 1,200 people, this site was almost unmanageable. Both branded and generic products were being manufactured here. It was important to identify ways to get the manufacturing costs down as well as upgrade outdated equipment. The team hoped to switch product lines more quickly using the same equipment. Kansas City was not receptive to the team approach.
- **Laval:** The facilities at Laval were very efficient but contained outdated equipment. This site needed to determine how to transfer production from Richmond Hill to Laval without losing supply continuity.
- **Hirakata:** The challenge at this site was meeting the stringent Japanese sanitary and product quality rules within the plant while at the same time introducing high-speed lines for production. The Japanese liked to inspect all products by sight and manual handling as opposed to using infrared scanners.
- **Anagni:** The team hoped to introduce high-speed lines in Anagni, where government oversight of job security permeates every decision. The high-speed lines would allow one person to monitor a packaging operation whereas up to eight had been necessary.

INITIAL DIFFICULTIES AND RESULTANT LEARNING

The global team encountered a variety of difficulties as it began. Members soon became aware that many site managers were the wrong members for this team for the following reasons:

- There was an atmosphere of politics, fear of loss of control, and fear of looking inadequate in front of others.
- Peers interfered with clear and open communication.
- Site managers were not always the most technically knowledgeable.

Team members also agreed that the global headquarters agenda could not supersede the needs of the sites. Initially the members saw the head-

BUILDING SWIFT TRUST AND STRONG NORMS

quarters agenda as an attempt to force consistency. They quickly agreed that forced consistency would not be good for all the sites. The team also got management to agree not to cut jobs during the global team's operation. This action helped gain trust from company employees for the global team.

The team recognized that an outside facilitator (see Chapter 9) would be necessary to run team meetings so that all members could participate freely. The initial attempt of having headquarters staff participate and facilitate had interfered with progress and acceptance.

It was also discovered that moving the team meetings around to different geographic sites was valuable. This practice allowed members to showcase their own site. Moreover, having the meetings take place away from headquarters developed a stronger sense of camaraderie. Team members became intimately aware of the dynamics affecting the other sites and abandoned the stigmas and stereotypes they had about each other—which led in turn to common understanding and greater trust. As members gained an appreciation for the plight of various sites, they eliminated their preoccupation with "one method to fit all situations."

Initially the global team spent a lot of time establishing team norms and investing in knowing each other—a process that paid off handsomely in the long term. Also, decisions were not forced or hurried. Although this approach created some concern on the part of management early on, in the long run decisions flowed much more freely.

Perhaps because an early "norming" period was adhered to, all team members were made equal. Rank, position, and size of site were left at the door. In the long term, the less experienced but more creative engineers proved to be, in many respects, the most influential members of the team.

There was other valuable learning as well: All ideas are team ideas; all technology is team technology; and uniformity is not a necessity. Technology team members also developed an understanding among themselves that each site's success would become the responsibility of all members of the technology team. This recognition proved important in minimizing competition among team members attempting to "show each other up."

As a side benefit, staff from different sites became known to each other, resulting in many job rotations. Getting to know one another and building trust was perhaps the most significant impact on employee relations.

OUTCOMES AND SUCCESSES

Thanks to the efforts of the global team, every site became a high-performing production site. Communications were improved and common ground was found. The global technology team modeled nonthreatening, open discussions and an integrated approach to dealing with manufacturing challenges instead of each site being concerned only for itself. The global team also removed the "U.S. is superior" notion that had resulted in high walls being built around sites to protect turf.

Production levels, cost of production (as a percentage of cost of goods), and speed of production processes all improved within the first year. And within three years, the commercial and business people were able to measure the global team's positive impact.

SWIFT TRUST: DIFFICULT BUT IMPERATIVE

On one level, it's easy to recognize that members of a global team must trust one another. Acknowledging that a high level of trust among team members reduces feelings of uncertainty and increases productivity seems a fairly simple idea to understand.

It is quite a difficult task, however, to implement swift trust as an integral component of the global team. Usually the trouble lies in the rigid structure of organizations. Global enterprises tend to hold a tight grip on information and levels of authority, leaving little room for innovation in team management. Most organizations are built around the assumption that people cannot be trusted, even in small matters. Employees, it is assumed, need to be monitored and controlled at all times. Today's global economy also presents new challenges, specifically for global teams. How do you trust team members located in very different (and often very distant) parts of the globe—people you cannot see?

In using the word *trust*, organizations really mean confidence—confidence in someone's competence and their commitment to a goal. Such trust among team members (wherever they are located) is absolutely imperative. The essential—indeed, indispensable—requirement of trust is the key that motivates other team members to continue their work conscientiously and with the team goal in mind. Without confidence, global team members quickly lose morale and motivation.

GUIDELINES FOR DEVELOPING SWIFT TRUST

Building trust on a global team is no easy task. But despite the difficulties, it can still be accomplished. A number of important guidelines have been developed for building trust on a global team—guidelines that can be put into practice by all types of global teams. If they are incorporated into the team's attitudes and work practices, trust is likely to grow swiftly among team members. The five guidelines for building trust in a global team are:

- Orientation
- Communication
- Clarity of vision
- Cultural sensitivity
- Disciplined work processes

Orientation

While recognizing that time constraints and geographic limitations are inherent in global teams, an orientation where members meet one another is not only necessary but critical. Put simply: Nothing can replace the face-to-face introduction of team members. Especially when travel resources are limited for geographically dispersed teams, the initial gathering of team members should be the first order of business (Devereaux and Johansen, 1994). Ignoring this step has serious consequences. Among others, it prevents the team from transforming "us" and "them" into "we."

Worksheet 3 presents a sample agenda for the first meeting. During the first meeting the team needs to develop ground rules—including the initiating of a mission statement, a charter, and norms of interaction. By the second meeting the team needs to have agreed on its mission, its charter, its norms of interaction regarding communication and technology use, and team roles.

WORKSHEET 3

Components and Procedures for Creating a Global Team Charter

Directions: This worksheet lists the topics that should be covered at the first team meeting. This can serve as the basis for creating an agenda for your own team. The chart includes a space for you to indicate who will be responsible for each issue and the amount of time you will allot to this issue.

TOPIC	MEMBERS	TIME
Agenda Explain the goals of the meeting and the expected outcomes. Solicit changes that team members would like to make in the agenda. Change the agenda accordingly. (This agenda should be sent at least a week before the meeting via e-mail. Changes can be suggested before the meeting as well as during the first session.)		
Introductions Ask members to describe themselves briefly. Provide guidelines on the type of information to share (name, role in the organization, last project worked on, similar projects worked on, time in the organization). To model the introduction (time and content), team leaders should introduce themselves first.		
Goals and mission Review the team's goals and mission that have been set by the organization. Provide a forum for team members' feedback on mission and statement. Before the next meeting summarize the information gathered, e-mail the review to team members, and ask for feedback. Present and finalize the mission at the next meeting.		
Initiate charter Introduce the elements of the charter you would like to see developed in the team (see Worksheet 2). Ask team members for written answers to specific charter issues before the next meeting. (Give a specific and realistic deadline.) Summarize and report on team members' feedback at the next meeting. Finalize the charter at the next meeting.		

BUILDING SWIFT TRUST AND STRONG NORMS

TOPIC	MEMBERS	TIME
Norms Hold a preliminary discussion of ground rules for team members' behavior. Set preliminary norms. Revisit these norms at the third or fourth meeting. (This allows time for team members to interact and then reflect on the interaction.) This preliminary discussion should include a review of technological plans and communication norms and plans.		
Discuss team work and deadline Provide information on the team's critical work and deadlines.		
Review work expectations for next meeting Review the mission, charter, and team work assignments and specific due dates. Send e-mail reminding members of these expectations and dates.		
Review meeting and evaluate Give members written and verbal feedback on what went well in the meeting, what could be improved, and specific suggestions for improvement. Allow team members to evaluate the team's process and the work.		

Between meetings it's a good idea to provide notes reviewing the issues discussed at the last meeting, major decisions made, and action steps with their deadlines and the person responsible. These notes should be shared within three days.

Programming "bonding time" into all face-to-face meetings is crucial too. People are more likely to build relationships and trust when they're in proximity, whereas tasks can be done at a distance. What's more, team members should be introduced into the planning of activities, no matter how little time the schedule may allow (Young 1998a, 1998b). Dinners, luncheons, and other activities that give team members a chance to know one another help to cement personal relationships. Whatever the activity, these personal encounters are invaluable in building trust—and are ultimately invested back into the team. Activities may include social

TABLE 5
Orientation Activities for Global Team Members

ACTIVITIES	DESCRIPTION
Competency development	Have the whole team engage in an instructional activity regarding a skill or knowledge set it needs to ensure the project's success—for example, instruction on technology, communication process, project management, or content subject of the team.
Social activity	Arrange a dinner or luncheon activity in which team members meet face-to-face—especially helpful if they sample foods of all the nationalities represented on the team.
Workplace introductions (virtual or face-to-face)	Have members take the team through a tour of their site—either through actual visits or through technology. A virtual introduction might include videoconferences or short videos developed by team members concerning their work sites.
Cultural introductions (virtual or face-to-face)	Have team members introduce their national cultures. Like the workplace introductions, these too can be done on-site or through technology.

interactions, developmental training, and workplace and cultural interactions. Table 5 suggests a range of orientation activities.

Communication

The value of communication should not be underestimated. Implementing effective methods of communication, tailored to the needs of a global team, should be thought out well in advance. Maintaining the lines of communication within the team must be a high priority. But communication is not spontaneous; it requires a conscious, ongoing effort on the part of every team member. People should be encouraged to contact others. Discussion and consultation—even on minor issues—can contribute to the collaborative action of the team. Through constant interaction, team members learn that they are on-track, have confidence they will be alerted to problems, and avoid serious setbacks to team goals.

Equally important, the art of communication includes designating specific roles of responsibility. Assignments for each team member have to be clear to the entire team and documented at the outset so there's no room for confusion or finger-pointing later on. In short, there can never be too much communication among team members. If possible, regular face-to-face team get-togethers should be scheduled. They not only allow the team to iron out difficulties but are helpful in aligning priorities as well (Young, 1998a, 1998b). Chapter 9 reviews the process of creating effective communication in global teams with the guidance of facilitators.

GLOBAL TEAM NORMS AND COMMUNICATION AT ERNST & YOUNG

Laurie Friedman

What enabled their global team to develop swift trust and strong team norms? Ernst & Young global team members responded to this question in a variety of ways:

- **Plan ahead:** Spend time planning for potential risk and obstacles. "Up-front homework makes the difference."

- **Communicate:** It is important to communicate, communicate, communicate! This cannot be overemphasized. Without face-to-face contact, the team needs constant communication. For example, the project manager follows all e-mails with scheduled phone calls. She sends group e-mails every week to maintain momentum and keep the lines of communication open.

- **Build in accountability:** This project comes from the top down. It is a high-level priority. Everyone knows that they will be accountable for their tasks at the end of the project.

- **Set deadlines:** Create tight deadlines and maintain them. Working in global teams is slow work.

- **Structure:** Build a framework for communication and troubleshooting ahead of time. Team members have competing demands. Most members are working on other projects. Be sensitive to these demands. The project manager on this team created a separate notebook for each country—allowing for careful tracking of issues for individual countries.

- **Get commitment:** Without members' commitment, the project will fail. Working on global teams requires extra energy and commitment. Even though England volunteered to join this team, they have been less cooperative than the other member countries. They are experiencing organizational changes including budget cuts, they are swamped with work, and they seem slightly uncomfortable with the team—all of which has impacted productivity and may ultimately be traced to the lack of acceptance from the beginning.
- **E-mail:** Be very careful how you write your e-mail messages. E-mail can easily be misinterpreted. Personalities, frustration, and annoyance can shine through. Spend time writing your e-mail messages, and reread them not only for accuracy but also for tone, expression, and ambiguity. There is less opportunity for derailment if you're careful of the messages you send and how they might be interpreted. E-mail messages reflect the personalities of team members. The project manager thought England's e-mail messages were dry, formal, and polite. Australia's were bubbly, talkative, lively. Different styles evolved as the team worked together. The project manager utilized the return receipt option—which allowed her to track e-mail messages and let member countries know "we know you got the e-mail and we're waiting for your reply."
- **Maintenance:** Keep everyone informed. Seventy percent of the work is organizational. One of the deliverables for this project, for example, required monthly head count data for each country. This measurement created a great deal of concern for one team member. Above all the member worried about how the data were going to be used. But the project manager was able to qualify the information and get the project back on track.
- **Learn as you go:** Be flexible, and stay aware of what is happening within the group.
- **Keep all appropriate parties informed:** Initially the project manager communicated with the project sponsors every three weeks. As the project progressed, however, she realized the importance of keeping the sponsors informed so that if problems arose they would be able to troubleshoot swiftly. She began sending weekly status reports to keep the key sponsors in touch with logistical issues.

- **Context:** It's important to understand the contextual issues that may affect a team member's ability to achieve the team's goals. Everybody is juggling multiple tasks that require various amounts of effort and time constraints. There are constellations of issues, both personal and professional, that may hinder the project's outcome if they are not discussed.

The most productive global teams are those whose members enjoy working with one another so much that they want to do it again. Successful groups see trust as the glue of the virtual workplace. Whenever possible, therefore, global groups should have some face-to-face time. When it comes to building trust, face-to-face relationships have no equal—not even electronic communication systems with all their bells and whistles.

We're learning that informal, spontaneous talk adds value. It not only builds trust, which motivates people to work collaboratively, but it also absorbs the shocks of conflict and misunderstanding and creates opportunities for mentoring, modeling, and monitoring. Every get-together of a global team, beginning with its first, can benefit from structured work periods and then some free time for socializing and fun. Grove and Hallowell (1998) discovered that during formal meetings, productive teams discussed relationships and emotions much more than unproductive teams did. Productive teams were both task-oriented and relationship-oriented. Unproductive teams were merely task-oriented.

Here's a way of keeping face-to-face relationships firmly in members' minds during time apart: Create for every member an identical wall map of the world with each person's photo and bio attached at the appropriate location.

Clarity of Vision

Once there has been an orientation meeting and the means of communication are clear, a global team should outline its purpose and goals and link them to the context of the corporate vision. (See Chapter 4.) Throughout the life of the team, the explanation of team goals may need clarification and feedback (Devereaux and Johansen, 1994). Clarity of vision involves frequent feedback, participant discussion, and reaching consensus on the common objective. Rather than pursuing objectives independently, members must be reminded that they are part of a collaborative effort—thus reinforcing their sense of community and common purpose (Young, 1998a, 1998b).

Cultural Sensitivity

Trust varies from culture to culture. As we noted in Chapter 2, cultures differ in how they communicate, how they relate, and how they show trust. Directness and honesty, for example, which may be seen as a way of showing trust in another person, in fact may create resentment and hence be less trust-enhancing. It may also be perceived as highly competitive, adversarial, and impersonal to those accustomed to a more indirect style of communication. On the other hand, indirectness may maintain a cordial relationship—but at the risk of misunderstanding that destroys trust later on.

Team members must therefore be alert, knowledgeable, and accepting of cultural differences. Participants must have the ability to practice cross-cultural skills and be willing to suspend judgment of different cultures. This approach is invaluable—and adds to the cohesion of the team (Grove and Hallowell, 1998). Those insensitive to cultural factors should not be included on a global team.

To overcome cultural differences and learn to work on a multicultural team, every member must participate in the process. They do so together by seizing the opportunity to learn about different cultures. Cultural learning involves such concepts as individualism versus collectivism, communication styles, and how and why a member's culture influences the team. By discussing cultural issues up front, team members avoid miscommunication—which can arise from seemingly small issues such as the slowness of Japanese to respond versus the American preference for quick answers to e-mails (Grove and Hallowell, 1998).

The chance to work with people from different cultures is in fact one of the most memorable and rewarding aspects of being associated with a global team. The goal is to develop team relationships and ways of doing business that all the members find practical and acceptable.

BUILDING SWIFT TRUST AND STRONG NORMS

Disciplined Work Processes

"Disciplined work processes" means doing what you planned to do. For trust to evolve on a team, the work processes that were outlined and stressed at the creation of the team must be carried out. The team's operational style must be consistent. When the meeting agenda has been set, it must be adhered to. The team vision must be followed. Consensus-style resolutions to problems must be practiced. For example, when certain channels of communication are deemed practical, they must be utilized (Grove and Hallowell, 1998). This does not mean the team cannot decide to reevaluate its means of communication. That is part of the team-building process. If team members decide on a change, the alternate method must be made clear to everyone and then be put into effect immediately. In other words, adoption of disciplined work processes means that the decisions reached must be implemented by all team members.

BUILDING TRUST AND NORMS AT MARRIOTT INTERNATIONAL

Jim O'Hern, Vice-President, Training and Organization Development

Marriott International is a leading worldwide hospitality company with over 2,000 operating units in the United States and fifty-two other countries and territories. Marriott has had a long history of using global teams. They are seen as a key leverage resource across business units. Marriott requires teams that are multilevel—region, business, and brands. What's more, teams enable the company to apply standards in a consistent way. Teams are also used for training purposes—that is, sharing ideas and people across units for learning as well as for solving problems.

The Marriott International lodging senior leadership team has been working together for over ten years and now handles a combination of staff and market functions. Over the years different members have been added. Members include area vice-presidents from Costa Rica, Hawaii, Kuala Lumpur, China, Australia, Washington, Frankfurt, London, Dubai, Miami, and Hong Kong. They speak a number of languages including Dutch, German, and Mandarin Chinese. Membership includes both men and women from a variety of functions including marketing, legal, revenue management, public relations, systems, human relations, finance, accounting, sales, engineering, operations, loss prevention, and training.

A major responsibility of the global team is to develop consistent application of Marriott standards and practices and thus further a corporate culture for businesses around the world. The second key purpose is to learn how Marriott can localize these procedures and thereby enhance the development of the business in each geographic area and culture.

The global leadership team meets face-to-face every quarter, and meetings are rotated throughout the different regions of the world. Outside guests, such as Marriott employees in various staff functions and specialists from local universities, are occasionally invited to these meetings.

Marriott's global leadership team operates under eight principles that guide its efforts:

1. Corporate leadership drives global growth, provides overall strategic direction, and ensures effective execution of all functions at all levels (corporate, region, area, business unit).

2. Each region provides leadership, drives growth, ensures owner satisfaction, and oversees compliance with hotel standards.

3. The area team (German, Singaporean) guides and supports the business units, links them to the company, and ensures compliance. Each team works for the local owner as well as for future owners.

4. The focus of each level is on accountability of results with an emphasis on revenue.

5. Decision making should be efficient, minimize bureaucracy, and reside at the level closest to the hotel.

6. Area and region teams are responsible for developing managers to meet current and future needs.

7. The structure is consistent within each region.

8. Corporate communications and brand/core initiatives require leadership from line management.

BUILDING SWIFT TRUST AND STRONG NORMS

TRUST, NORMS, AND COHESION

The guidelines for building swift trust among members of a global team will weld the team into a cohesive unit. When members know one another as the result of orientation, when face-to-face relationships are established, when the channels of communication open for team members to use comfortably and frequently—then misunderstandings and setbacks are avoided. As team members work together to define and commit themselves to the goals and purpose of the team, they become bonded by a common vision and identity. Finally, when the team's cultural differences are recognized and discussed, the diversity adds significantly to the rewards of participating on a global team.

In this chapter we've examined how global teams can develop the swift trust necessary to become effective quickly—before the impact of distance, cultural differences, and time pressures tears the team apart. The successes of MMD and Marriott demonstrate the importance of trust in building team cohesiveness and commitment.

Part Three

CULTURAL AND TECHNOLOGICAL FOUNDATIONS

Chapter 6

Capturing the Power of Cultural Diversity

Global teams have members from diverse cultures and cultural backgrounds. Culture, which forms the way we think and act, causes team members to see reality very differently. The diversity in multicultural teams has the potential for friction, misunderstanding, and tension that, left unattended, can quickly result in disintegration and conflict—a factor often cited by global companies as a prime reason for their reluctance to use global teams unless there is absolutely no other option.

A major challenge for global teams therefore becomes how to encourage and tap into the rich experiences of people with their wide-ranging perspectives and ways of acting—but in a way that does not have the group end up in chaotic conditions with little or no results. In short, the challenge is this: How can we achieve a balance between fostering the healthy conflict of ideas while controlling cultural differences among team members?

In this chapter we examine how global teams can, in fact, develop a strong sense of global unity and at the same time utilize the powerful synergy generated by cultural diversity. We illustrate the global/cultural integration synergy through an analysis of Boeing's global team in the Czech Republic. As we will see throughout the book, all the other components of the GlobalTeams Model must be employed in order to maintain the global integration and cohesiveness needed by global teams.

VALUING CULTURAL DIVERSITY

There are a number of strategies a team can undertake to build a common purpose and operating practices and yet allow cultural differences. The first step is company management's obligation to create corporate-wide values such as "all cultures are equal in this organization." Karen Ward (1999) cites four main components of this multicultural outlook: widespread acceptance of cultural diversity; low levels of prejudice; positive mutual attitudes among cultural groups; and creating a sense of attachment to the larger system. Developing this type of culture is an ongoing process. It demands continual evaluation, reengineering, and development.

The diversity generated by multiculturalism creates great power for an organization due to its tremendous potential of bringing in fresh ideas and perspectives needed to solve problems, design products, or think about new processes. But cultural diversity also has the potential to create chaos, disharmony, and disintegration—which, unless harnessed, can damage organizations as well as the team and its members.

To gain the benefits of cultural diversity, team members need to receive training in the principles and theories behind culture. Although American companies spend over $100 billion a year in workplace training, very little of this is spent on cross-cultural preparation and programs. In this respect, the United States is far behind Asia and Europe in preparing employees to work on global teams. Two key facts:

- Some 70 percent of American businesspeople who work on overseas programs are given no cultural training or preparation.

- Yet these same American companies lose over $2 billion a year due to inadequate cross-cultural guidance for their employees in multicultural situations (Marquardt, 1999).

Too many American businesses simply assume that American ways and business practices are the norm. They seem to think a manager or sales representative or team member who is successful in Boston will be just as successful in Bangkok. Nothing could be further from the truth!

Akio Morita, former chairman of Sony, commented that "culture may impact products, services, and operations by only 10 percent, but this is the most important 10 percent." This 10 percent may determine the success or failure of a global team. Like a growing number of global leaders, Morita recognized the crucial importance of having people throughout the organization who are effective in the various cultures in which the company operates.

People and companies around the world think, act, work, learn, and lead in differing ways based upon the cultural environment. Culture consciously and subconsciously shapes our values, assumptions, perceptions, and behavior. It sets systematic guidelines for how we should conduct our thinking, our actions, our rituals, and our business.

These value differences explain why people of varying cultures tend to act differently within global teams when it comes to leadership, learning, communication, and work. In Chapter 2 we cited numerous challenges faced by global teams because of cultural differences. Let's look at how global team leaders and members can manage these differences in a way that allows them to benefit from cultural diversity.

GROUPINGS

Ideally, the makeup of global teams is diverse in order to maximize various perspectives and obtain fresh viewpoints. Though diversity is sought, it is important that group members have roughly the same level of competence so they feel comfortable in challenging one another. Mixing people of differing ages, genders, roles, and the like fits in with the Western values of egalitarianism, equality, and informality. Americans like variety, different perspectives, new ideas, and the give-and-take among differing groups. Competence is more important than rank or status.

In most other cultures, however, mixing people of differing status groups violates their sense of hierarchy and acceptance of differences. Mixing may be seen as a means of undermining authority in the workplace. It may even cause embarrassment, confusion, and loss of face. In some cultures, young people in a group will hesitate to speak out if older people are in the group—in this case, age may be seen as more important than competence. A person's status determines the degree to which he can state his opinion. In many societies, there is a rigid, hierarchical, bureaucratic structure with great status differences and extreme deference to authority. And in some conservative Islamic cultures, men and women cannot even be in the same room, much less exchange ideas on an equal level.

Cultures that appreciate hierarchy and clear roles have trouble bringing together differing groups. Seating arrangements are determined by status. Language conventions dictate that one be addressed in a superior or inferior fashion. Formality, especially among those of differing status, is absolutely essential.

Conversely, the collectivism of other cultures encourages working in global teams. Such cultures value teamwork and solving problems as a group. Thus action learning groups fit better in these cultures than the individualism of Western cultures. (According to Hofstede's [1991] studies, the United States has the highest individualism of any culture.) The Hispanic sense of machismo can also indicate individualistic tendencies.

Cultures can be differentiated by the distance considered acceptable for conversing and conducting business. Americans like to be between 18 and 36 inches away in communicating (the distance of an outstretched arm). This is much too far for Latin Americans and Arabs, who like to be within 18 inches and touch. Asians are uncomfortable when they're within 3 feet. This is why Germans and Americans shake hands when greeting, Egyptians and Brazilians hug, and Japanese and Thai bow.

Tips

- Be culturally and politically sensitive to fellow team members.
- In many cultures, a person's status in the group continues to determine the degree to which they can state their opinions. Mixing people of differing cultural status may severely limit their participation.
- In a similar vein, some cultures encourage verbal comments by the leader of the group but not the individual participants.
- Recognize hierarchy and the status of members.
- Build on the cultural values of working in groups (collectivism).
- Begin with some team-building activities to assist members in becoming comfortable with and supportive of one another.

COMMUNICATIONS

Communications can range from high-context (environment and nonverbal cues do much of the communication) to low-context (the words themselves are the primary locus of communication). When developing a global team communication strategy, it's important to consider the amount of context available through different types of interaction. A person-to-person contact, for example, may cover a whole range of possible interactions: informal contact (in the hallway outside a meeting); a physical exchange (handshake or bow); nonverbal cues (facial expressions, gestures); immediate feedback; voice tone; and more.

Communications also range from expressive to instrumental. These different styles of communication result in enormous cultural variability—ranging from exaggeration of desire or intent in the Middle East to silence and pauses during interactions as in Asian cultures.

Because of these differences, asking for feedback and encouraging self-analysis may be fine for Westerners who value frankness and openness. But it could be disastrous in Asia where a much higher value is placed on concealing your feelings and not prying into the thoughts of others. In some cultures you must not offer advice in a public setting. Pointing out a weakness is difficult in Spanish-speaking cultures since people are not expected to speak negatively of others. For Arabs, "Allah loveth not the speaking ill of anyone." Hence you may have trouble getting accurate information, especially the bad news. For example, members of some Asian cultures may be reluctant to tell us that things are going wrong.

Tips

- Remember that a high-context person will find a low-context person's directness uncomfortable and even rude. A low-context person will often find a high-context person shifty, hard to read, and unclear.

- In elaborate cultures, speakers are expected to produce rich and expressive language, often through the elaborate use of metaphors and similes. In instrumental cultures, the speaker is expected to use silences and pauses and understatement.

- In personal-style cultures, status takes a back seat to informality. But in a contextual-style culture, the speaker's status and role are paramount.

- Communications should follow explicit protocols, commonly understood definitions of business processes, jargon, and cultural symbols (Devereaux and Johansen, 1994, p. 153). Chinese, for example, have highly formalized business communications whereas Americans are more informal.

- Be aware of the cultural priorities of "being clear" and "being polite." Polite cultures are concerned about hurting feelings, minimizing imposition, avoiding negative evaluation by the other person. Clear cultures want clarity and effectiveness.

- Criticism may be taken very personally in many cultures. Personal relationships can become strained if the criticized person loses face.

- Avoid forcing people to respond with a "no." Rather than using yes-and-no questions, try using contextual cues to assess the level of agreement or disagreement.

- Recognize that members may base their response on what they think you want rather than what they actually think.

- People from a direct culture will need to develop a high tolerance for ambiguity when working in an indirect culture.

- Holding continued direct eye contact is considered rude in many Asian cultures.

USING E-MAIL AND VIDEOCONFERENCING WITH ERNST & YOUNG'S GLOBAL TEAMS

Laurie Friedman

Unlike as in face-to-face and phone communications, Americans using e-mail tend to be less polite—presumably because they have low awareness of the other's social presence. The result was a faster escalation of conflicts that we easily recognized as detrimental to team success.

CAPTURING THE POWER OF CULTURAL DIVERSITY

In our global team, e-mail users were less aware of each other's prestige and experience, as well, presumably because these don't show up on a screen. As a result, e-mail conversations and debates were more inclusive and less inhibited by age and rank. That's good, right? Not so fast. We're talking about geographically dispersed, multicultural teams here. Outside the United States, people are not as enamored of inclusiveness as we are; they give far more respect to status and hierarchy. Believe it or not, our egalitarian tendencies can perplex and offend them.

American team members complained that team members abroad, such as the Japanese, were slow to respond to e-mails and faxes—an example of how e-mail, which reflects Americans' need for speed, collides with the social features of Japanese culture. Leaving aside the fact that the Japanese are using a second language, let's note first that their language does not include the concept of "spontaneous." Japanese are correct and proper and expect to craft their responses carefully.

Moreover, Japanese members needed to develop consensus within their group before replying. For the Japanese, a written message devoid of social and other contextual information is an incomplete message. Americans like the efficiency of targeted, spare prose. But for the Japanese and others it's often not enough to compel action.

Videoconferencing falls short, too. One of the American members, while in Taiwan, participated in a videoconference between local team members and Americans back in the United States. When a U.S.-based member noisily pounded the desk while arguing a point, the American in Taiwan sensed an abrupt change in the locals' demeanor signaling that they had taken offense. This reaction was not noticed by the Americans in the United States. Fortunately, over the next several days, the Taiwan-based American was able to act as a culture broker and soothe the locals' consternation.

LANGUAGE

English has become the global language. More than a billion people are able to speak it. For most people in the world, however, English is a second or third language, and many members of the global team may have trouble understanding when it's spoken quickly. When using English with these group members, it may be advisable to provide a translator or at least make every effort to speak clearly and slowly to ensure that your messages are being fully transmitted.

Tips

- If you are unable to speak the local language, at least try to learn some of the basic phrases (good morning, thank you). Teammates will be pleased with your interest in their language.

- If the meetings are being conducted in English, be sure to carefully assess the group's language ability and respond accordingly. Do not assume that they understand you or the company materials. Be sensitive to their difficulties in comprehending. Avoid colloquialisms or jargon unless you carefully define and explain them.

- Concentrate on speaking slowly and clearly. Remember that the American accent may be hard to understand for Indians, East Africans, and others who speak British dialects.

- Use visuals as often as possible. Overhead transparencies, graphics, and pictures will make it easier for your teammates to follow you. To ensure understanding, you may need to reinforce key points.

- Recognize that meetings will take longer. Schedule frequent breaks. Don't rush—you'll only wind up wasting time later restating and explaining information you thought you had covered.

- Encourage team members to speak, and give them reinforcement when they do. This will help them become comfortable using their non-native language.

- Distribute written reports in advance when appropriate. This will give non-English speakers time to prepare and gain a better understanding if the materials are not in their local language.

- Be patient and listen carefully. Respect their efforts to convey concepts and feelings in another language (and hence in another cultural context).

- Don't worry about the occasional silences. The silence may be related to members' cultural behavior, or maybe they are taking time to translate and think in English—two time-consuming processes.

- It may be wise to allow team members, while working in small groups, to converse in their own language and to prepare a flipchart summary, also in their native language. When presenting to the whole group, the speaker can then translate the summary into English.

LEADERSHIP ROLES AND EXPECTATIONS

In Chapter 3 we looked at the key skills of leaders of global teams. Here we consider how culture impacts the practice and acceptance of the leadership role. Based on their cultural background and organizational experiences, people tend to lead in different ways and expect their leaders to act in certain ways. Many Westerners prefer a participative, democratic style of leadership while people in many other cultures prefer a manager who is much more clear and directive.

Tips

- Recognize that leadership roles and ways of being effective vary from culture to culture and will affect the manner in which teams work and are led.

- In a hierarchical culture it may be difficult for senior-level members to work for a leader who lacks a high-level title, education, or status.

- Different cultures have different protocols and action chains for reporting to managers, especially foreign managers.

- From the beginning, explain your expectations of yourself as a leader and the members as members. Try to be specific about behavior rules—how you wish to be addressed, how you will address them, and your expectations.

TIME

Time is seen by Americans as a precious resource they can control. "Time is money" and "Don't waste time" are dictums we hear from early childhood onward. What's more, our concept of time is fixed; there is a sense of punctuality, deadlines, and urgency. Meetings begin on time and schedules are taken seriously.

This attitude toward punctuality is less prevalent in many other societies—especially in Latin America and the Middle East, where time is not worshiped in the same way. In these regions of the world, relationships are more important than promptness. Discussing an interesting point may be seen as more valuable than staying on schedule.

Tips

- When setting meeting times in another culture, there may be a number of differing expectations regarding the 9:00 A.M. start. In some cultural settings, when the schedule indicates 9:00 A.M. as the starting time, it may mean that no one arrives until then—and the true starting time will be 10:00 A.M. Other cultures take the 9:00 A.M. as absolute—and if a person is a few minutes late, team members may feel that he or she is not taking them seriously. In these situations, the team leader must determine which cultural definition of time will be employed—his or the group's—and then stick to it. Do not schedule too tightly; most groups want considerable time for discussion and exploring.

- Take into account the team's values, styles, and attitudes. It's unwise to limit team activities to fifteen minutes when the cultural perception of agreement is harmony and consensus, not majority rule.

- When scheduling meetings and meals, remember that different societies have different customs regarding the amount of time set aside for them. In most countries, it typically takes about one hour for lunch. In France, however, they expect two hours. In Spain, they take two or three hours—but then are willing to work until 8:00 P.M. Remember the important social values that eating provides for various cultures. If eating times cannot be compressed, try building activities into these long dinner sessions.

PROBLEM SOLVING AND SEEKING SOLUTIONS

All global teams spend much of their time solving problems and seeking creative solutions to the tasks they have been assigned. But the way in which these processes are undertaken varies from culture to culture. For example, the questioning/reflection process is more comfortable in cultures that value informality and egalitarianism—cultures where people can be more directive and challenging of each other. The Western approach of inductive thinking and problem solving encourages careful examination of the particular event and developing new ways of responding. Our approach of asking questions is built on the Socratic way of learning; it naturally leads to more openness and creativity in handling problems. Discussion tends to be logical and rational with little show of emotion.

Western culture encourages the discussion of personal as well as organizational problems in a public setting (frankness). It is okay for a Western manager to admit difficulties in solving a problem and thus be willing to turn it over to outsiders or subordinates. It is easier for him to trust subordinates and delegate power to them (egalitarianism).

Taking more time to question, reflect, and discuss would work well in Latin and Arabic cultures where time is flexible and there is less need to rush to results. The non-Westerner's cultural ability to listen carefully, to value and respect others, and to seek group consensus are key characteristics of the global team members. But in some cultures, such as China's, there is great impatience over spending too much time in discussion and reflection; there is a great desire for quick results and speed.

Finally, in some cultures it is more difficult for someone to turn over his most critical problems to a group or to subordinates. And even if the organization has delegated power to a team, some cultures would still not recognize this power unless the organizational leader were physically present.

Tips

- Remember that universalistic solutions are seen by many cultures as too simplistic, too naïve, and too American. Focus on the culturally sensitive, particularized, and tailor-made approaches.

- Recognize that not all cultures see change as a "necessary good." When appropriate, build upon the traditions of the past as well as the needs of the future.

- Be sensitive to the religious and cultural constraints as well as the need for harmony in developing solutions to problems.

BALANCING COMPETITIVE AND COOPERATIVE STYLES

What motivates workers? The answer differs significantly from culture to culture. How we work and learn with each other ranges from being very competitive to being cooperative. *Competitive* cultures emphasize being assertive and focus on results, success, and achievements—especially as they relate to tasks and rewards. Work is highly valued and determines one's worth, value, and importance. *Cooperative* cultures place a high value on consensual decision making. Employees are hired not only for their skills but also for their ability to fit into the group, promote its values, facilitate communication, demonstrate loyalty, and contribute to the overall work environment.

Recent research by Hampden-Turner and Trompenaars (1997) has found that East Asian cultures may, in fact, have several characteristics that make them better suited to work in teams. Westerners prefer playing what the researchers call a "finite game" in which you win or lose by specific criteria. Easterners, by contrast, play an "infinite game" in which all players learn cooperatively. Westerners prefer values such as winning, individualism, competition, universalism (rule by law), inner-directed, status achieved, and sequential time (time as a race). Easterners prefer values such as community, cooperating, outer-directed, status ascribed (the good should succeed), and particularism (unique and exceptional). In the finite game, improvement comes from the fiercer competitor rising to the top in a battle—the survival of the fittest. In the infinite game, improvement comes from the game itself—by developing "survival of the fittingest," players self-organize more effectively.

Tips

- Identify the motivating factors in the culture of team members.
- Develop activities that build on the workstyles of all the team members—and not necessarily on what motivates you.
- Competition between groups may be much more comfortable than competition within groups.

Now let's look at how Boeing's global team handled a variety of cultural challenges with their manufacturing project in Odolena Voda in the Czech Republic.

CULTURAL CHALLENGES WITH BOEING'S GLOBAL TEAM IN THE CZECH REPUBLIC

Michael Campolo, Senior Manager of Human Resources

Boeing, the world's largest maker of commercial jets, employs over 230,000 people worldwide, and 2000 sales were over $50 billion. Global teams are of immense importance to Boeing—in fact, hundreds of its global teams meet every day all over the world. A joint venture between Boeing and the Czech firm Aero Vodochody is an excellent example of how global teams are achieving important gains for Boeing.

The joint project is located in Odolena Voda, just outside the city of Prague in the Czech Republic. The Boeing Company holds a 34 percent stake in Aero Vodochody, the manufacturer of the L-159 advanced light attack combat aircraft. There are currently seventy-two aircraft on order from the Czech Republic government. In addition, the AE-270 (a single-engine plane carrying eight to ten passengers) and aircraft structure assemblies are being produced at this location.

The global teams were composed of Americans and Czech employees. Each of the Boeing team members had to make a minimum two-year commitment to the program, for which they relocated themselves and their families to the Czech Republic. One of the primary objectives for the global teams was to develop a cost management system at Aero Vodochody that included measures of success related to profitability and process improvements. Once these measures were developed, the global teams would develop the expertise to implement the cost management processes throughout the company.

At the start the global teams faced five major challenges:

1. The Czech Republic is dealing with many of the problems associated with an Eastern European firm moving from a state-controlled system to a market-driven economy. In the past, Aero Vodochody did not have to earn a profit. The company only needed to produce aircraft without worrying about costs. As a result, there were a number of inefficient practices including overstaffing.

2. "Single-point failure" was common in the organization since many complex work tasks belonged exclusively to individuals, and decisions got delayed and mistakes were made at these junctures.

3. The company had never used a timekeeping system for such analysis as earned value management. Its only purpose was to accurately pay employees according to their time cards.

4. Language barriers were troublesome, so interpreters were needed—which lengthened the amount of time necessary to hold a conversation. In addition, the context of the discussion was sometimes lost since the specific techniques to perform an operation are often difficult to describe through a third party.

5. Finally, there was the challenge of building the concept of teamwork itself. Since the country was formerly under communist rule, the work culture reflected a major difference from what the American workers were accustomed to. Teamwork among employees was virtually nonexistent, and now the global teams were attempting to create cultural changes in the workplace to build better teamwork. Moreover, the Boeing approach of utilizing multidisciplined teams was also new to Aero Vodochody.

The efforts of Boeing team members created a great deal of excitement among the employees. Of course, some people felt apprehension about the changes—after all, the corporate culture was being radically altered. It was also important for the Americans to recognize they could learn a great deal from the perspectives of their Czech colleagues that could benefit Boeing not only in the Czech Republic but elsewhere.

CAPTURING THE POWER OF CULTURAL DIVERSITY

The teams have been successful because many of the initial barriers were acknowledged and overcome. Both the organizational culture and work processes were changed. There was a great deal of trust created among the culturally diverse team members that resulted in high levels of cooperation. Working side by side on a global work team such as this, both parties gain from the experience. All members of the teams committed themselves to making the program a success. Finally, the learning gained from this program is being applied by Boeing in achieving its overall vision of having a single aerospace focus that operates on a global level.

UNIFYING THE DIVERSE GLOBAL TEAM

The greater the diversity of a global team, the greater the possibility it may unravel into confusion and conflict—unless there are factors that can be developed to bring integration to the team. Without some unifying factors, the global team will lose its identity and begin to disintegrate.

The centrifugal forces that create the benefits of diversity must be balanced by a centripetal force that curbs the tendency to drift into confusion and conflict. That centripetal force is globalization—which can harness all the powerful centrifugal forces of diversity.

What can global teams do to "globalize" themselves so that they have a universal force "strong enough to be tangible yet flexible enough to stretch and hold across distances and cultures" (Devereaux and Johansen, 1994, p. 146)? What factors are necessary for globalization to permeate teams?

First, globalization can occur as a result of an agreement on global principles and processes. This global integration also can come about through such highly controlling actions as policy manuals and regulations that are reinforced by aggressive management review. Or it can be achieved through mechanisms such as a shared vision and values that allow each element of the team to operate independently within the boundaries of the vision.

Global values that might serve as a cohesive force for global teams include:

- *Quality and continuous improvement*—commitment to providing the best possible quality to whatever the team develops

- *Speed and timeliness*—commitment to be responsive to the time demands of fellow members as well as to those of internal and external customers

- *Worklife and humanization*—appreciation of the family and other nonorganizational demands on the team

- *Collaboration*—commitment to cooperation rather than competition as the team's modus operandi

- *Global thinking*—ability to search for global perspectives and see global possibilities

- *Cultural sensitivity*—not only a tolerance but a dedicated interest in other cultures

- *Continuous learning*—appreciation that all members must be open to new ideas

- *Cultural customization*—recognition that customers seek products and services that apply to their tastes and situation

Stephen Rhinesmith (1996) emphasizes the necessity of a global mind-set on the part of all global team members. A global mind-set sees the world globally, is open to exchanging ideas across borders, is able to break down provincial ways of thinking. The emphasis is on balancing global and local needs—and being able to operate cross-functionally, cross-divisionally, and cross-culturally around the world.

Balancing Global Integration with Cultural Diversity

Davison and Ward (1999) have cited a number of cultural and organizational factors that affect the global team's environment and thus the interaction of team members and their effectiveness. The cultural factors include:

- Differences in the cultural norms of team members

- The degree to which different people manifest their cultural norms

- Differences in language fluency, communication patterns, nonverbal cues, and who says what and when

CAPTURING THE POWER OF CULTURAL DIVERSITY

- Culturally different leadership styles
- Different expectations about key team processes

The organizational factors are:

- The status of different cultures within the organization
- The geographic location of team members
- Differences between functional, professional, and other subcultures in the organization

These factors must be continually managed if the global team is to survive. They must be managed throughout the team's life cycle—including the first meetings, the midway point, and the closing stages. The earlier they are acknowledged and worked on, the easier the team's effort to achieve results. There is no way to prepare specifically for these factors. It's just a matter of being continually vigilant for these potential obstacles and developing contingency plans to deal with them.

Key Points When Working Across Cultures

Craig Storti (1991), a noted cross-cultural specialist, cites the following points as keys to working with the varying cultures of global teams:

- Don't assume sameness.
- Monitor your instincts—what may seem "natural" to you may in fact be cultural.
- "Familiar" behavior may have different meanings in different cultures.
- Don't assume that what you meant is what was understood.
- Don't assume that what you understood is what was meant.
- You don't have to like "different" behavior, but you should try to understand where it comes from.
- Most people behave rationally—you just have to find the rationale.

Managing the Cultural Dynamics in Global Teams

Instead of seeing the tension between cultural diversity and global integration as an unwelcome headache, try viewing it as the primary source of synergy that can contribute to the global team's energy and successes. Many companies have indeed synergized diversity without losing the unifying elements of leadership, vision, norms, and swift trust discussed in the previous three chapters.

Managing the global/cultural dynamic lies at the heart of creating and implementing a successful global team. In Chapter 7 we will explore the technological support that provides the critical framework for global teams—the nerve system that allows them to communicate and interact effectively across culture and distance in carrying out their work.

Chapter 7

Technological Support and Communications

Global teams must operate quickly and effectively across time and space. They cannot do this, however, without high levels of technological support. Technology has thus become absolutely critical for global teams carrying out basic team functions of communicating, making decisions, learning, building cohesiveness, and managing knowledge.

In this chapter we look at the four categories of technology that are available for a high-performing global team: communication technology, decision-making technology, information technology, and learning technology. We will discuss the first two types of technology together since communications and decision making are so intertwined. Later in the chapter we examine the use of technology in global teams at BP and IBM.

COMMUNICATION AND DECISION-MAKING TECHNOLOGY

Global teams need communication systems that effectively, efficiently, and easily allow them to share information and make decisions inside and outside the team over distance and time (Snow et al., 1996). Groupware, a type of technology that facilitates the work of groups

	SAME TIME "Synchronous"	DIFFERENT TIME "Asynchronous"
SAME PLACE "Co-located"	Voting, presentation support	Shared computers
DIFFERENT PLACE "Distance"	Videophones, chat	E-mail, workflow

Figure 5 • GROUPWARE

(communication, cooperation, coordination), can be categorized along two dimensions: according to *time*—whether team members are working together at the same time (synchronous) or at different times (asynchronous)—and according to *location*—whether team members are working together in the same place (co-located) or in different places (distance). (See Figure 5.)

Groupware facilitates communication, enables telecommuting, brings together multiple perspectives and expertise, saves time and money in coordinating group work, facilitates group problem solving, and enables structured interaction and anonymous interchanges. Specifically, this kind of collaborative technology helps global teams with three processes. First, it assists a team in gathering and presenting information. Tasks in this process include storing, processing, and retrieving information. Nonelectronic means include file cabinets, blackboards, and paper handouts. Electronic and computerized forms include electronic whiteboards and collaborative document management.

Second, technology supports teams by allowing them to show work to one another and share images with other team members. Tools such as telephones, videoconferencing, and shared whiteboards with electronic cursors can be used to convey information.

And third, technology helps teams with deliberations by enhancing their ability to brainstorm, solve problems, and make decisions. Technology enables a team to organize or model the actual information it is creating. Process structuring tools can help organize problems by prioritizing, ordering, or assigning action. GSS technologies, project management software, and group calendar software can assist with each of these processes (Mittleman and Briggs, 1999).

Groupware systems are designed to work in conjunction with one another—for example, group calendars are used to schedule videoconferences. Let's look at a variety of groupware applications, both asynchronous and synchronous.

Asynchronous Groupware

E-mail, the most common groupware application, is designed to allow two people to pass written messages to one another. Today basic e-mail systems include features for forwarding messages, filing messages, creating mailing groups, and attaching files to messages.

Newsgroups and mailing lists are used to send messages to large groups of people. Newsgroups show messages to a user when he requests it. A mailing list delivers messages as they become available.

Workflow systems allow for documents to be routed through a team through a relatively fixed process. Workflow systems usually provide features such as routing, development of forms, and support for differing roles and privileges.

Hypertext is a system that allows you to link text documents with one another. When several people author and link documents, the system lets others respond and edit each other's work. Hypertext systems allow people to see who has visited a certain page or link or see how a link has been followed.

Group calendars are systems that allow scheduling, project management, and coordination among many people and provide support for scheduling equipment.

Collaborative writing systems are word processors that provide asynchronous support by allowing a document to show authorship and allowing users to track changes and make annotations to the document. These systems sometimes help users to plan and coordinate the writing process by locking parts of the documents or linking separately authored documents. These systems may also be synchronous in that they allow team members to see each other's changes in real time.

Synchronous Groupware

Shared whiteboards allow groups to view and draw on a shared drawing surface even when they are at a distance. Sometimes the whiteboard indicates where each person is drawing by means of color-coded telepointers or by labels identifying each person.

Video communication, a telephone system with a visual component, allows for two-way or multi-way calling with live video.

Chat systems allow groups to write messages in real time in a public space. Rooms with controlled access or with moderators to lead the discussion may also form part of these systems.

Decision support systems are used to facilitate group decision making. They usually provide tools for brainstorming, critiquing ideas, assigning weights and probabilities to events or alternatives, and voting.

Intranets link an organization's computers in a closed network that is accessible to people within the organization. They are accessed by browsers.

*Keypad voting system*s are a mechanism that can tally the votes at a meeting.

Table 6 presents guidelines on when and where to use these different technologies in global teams as well as their respective advantages and disadvantages.

TABLE 6
Global Team Technologies

TECHNOLOGY	ADVANTAGES	DISADVANTAGES	GROUND RULES
Telephone	• Immediate answers or can defer call till later • Personal • Can choose any language • Can change tone and information halfway through	• Can be intrusive • No record or use of documents unless previously faxed • Variable global quality with echoes, crackles, delays • Long distances • 9–12-hour time differences inconvenient	• Keep to the point • Note main points before calling • Make notes during conversation
Teleconference	• Involves large group • Can impose disciplined communication • Don't have to book them like videoconferences yet they give you immediacy of response and the nuance of reactions missing in e-mail and fax	• Difficult to keep the whole group in mind • Have to select one language • Second-language speakers cannot use body language to interrupt or show confusion • Underused in global working	• Fax agenda beforehand, elect facilitator to keep time, stop wafflers, and involve everyone • Need to allow time for second-language speakers
Facsimile	• Very cheap but not secure when sent over the Internet • Good for accessing less-developed countries • Some people act on the written word rather than the spoken • Can send specifications, designs, pictures	• Cannot edit while sending • Frustrating if there's intermittent power failure, machine is switched off, or paper runs out • Needs good connection	• Stick to facts • Good for small amounts of urgent data • Can be sent and received direct from computer

TABLE 6 CONT'D
Global Team Technologies

TECHNOLOGY	ADVANTAGES	DISADVANTAGES	GROUND RULES
E-mail	• Excellent for short, encouraging personal messages and sorting out details • Can set up internal interest groups as well as broadcast progress and achievements • Can reach a specific or wide audience • Participants can choose when and how to respond and can edit received messages • Gives second-language speakers time to hone what they want to say • Lets you act when it suits you • Cheap, excellent tool using local servers in developing countries where phoning and postal mail are unreliable, expensive, and/or slow	• Usually confined to text unless participants have identical packages for sending attached files • Often lose formatting from work processing files • Not good for controversial announcements • Can be hard to set up the architecture between disparate sites and companies • American standards tend to dominate • Can be ignored • Overload • Overused • Messages may get lost and go unanswered • If too many questions, some tend to go unanswered • Loses intonation and subtlety • Don't use for urgent messages that need a reply—phone or walk to the person's office instead	• Use the priority and action codes • Give clear headings indicating the subject • Keep points clear and succinct • Avoid philosophical debates • Create company etiquette for expressing emotion and negative responses • Train newcomers in company idioms and slang • File and delete as you read • Make an address book of regular mails • Use very specific mailing lists for specific issues and keep them updated • Avoid general mailings

TABLE 6 CONT'D
Global Team Technologies

TECHNOLOGY	ADVANTAGES	DISADVANTAGES	GROUND RULES
External e-mail	• No need for company to invest in own LANs and architecture • Great for informal chats at low cost • Can access wide range of resources at low cost	• Loose formatting or attachments become scrambled in different coding • Viruses can be carried on attachments • Not secure	• Same practices as above • Use filter for junk mail • Remove attachment before sending replies
Internet	• Can access wide range of information at low cost • Teams can create web sites to stimulate interest in suppliers and customers not on internal architecture	• Can pick up viruses • Time consuming—especially if surfing is nonspecific • Companies can limit its usefulness by vetting all mail to stop surfing on company time	• Update company access to latest web-search facilities • Keep web site graphics, colors, and logos to a minimum • Limit or log connection time and probably access to certain sites—especially if offices are still closed-door
Group decision support system	• Can increase quantity (not necessarily quality) of participation from all participants • Can dramatically cut meeting time • Focus the discussion on task	• Anonymity may not suit all cultures • Does not develop personal relationships • Has more impact in teams of more than eight people	• Facilitator must be competent with technology and group processes

TABLE 6 CONT'D
Global Team Technologies

TECHNOLOGY	ADVANTAGES	DISADVANTAGES	GROUND RULES
Groupware products (such as Lotus Notes)	• Allow team to consolidate contributions into one document • Allow preferential editing/reading access • Enable point-to-point online screen shows	• Can have problems setting up and maintaining the technology—especially between high-level and low-level infrastructure sites • Large investment in training and online coaching is needed to make full use of it • Need good in-house people to create customized templates • All users need to be in All-Lotus desktop environment to take advantage of team computing capabilities	• Be selective about edit, read only, and access options • Create process and chat files alongside technical and data files • Teach team members how to customize their own files
Whiteboards/ shared database	• Excellent record of team activities	• Can be hard to file and index so that information is accessible • Somebody has to maintain relevance—which may lead to reduced usefulness	• Need disciplined updating and sending of information • Information must be usefully packaged • Someone needs to be responsible for editing the site

TABLE 6 CONT'D
Global Team Technologies

TECHNOLOGY	ADVANTAGES	DISADVANTAGES	GROUND RULES
Group video-conferencing	• Can see more than teleconferencing—and group can all be looking at the same written text, so greater reliability and relevance can be assessed	• Unspontaneous, formal • Delayed actions due to small bandwidths • Many people say this is not much better than teleconferencing—unless simultaneous data exchange is also possible • Size of room and access may differ between sites • Needs booking • Still expensive	• Need advance planning; agendas and preparation; clear outcomes; process facilitator (e.g., speak one at a time, not more than two minutes); clear bulleted decisions and actions • Have technician on hand for new teams
Desktop video-conferencing	• More spontaneous • Adds personal and immediate dimensions—allows you to interrupt and change input in response to visual cues • No need to travel or gather at specific sites	• Still not as rich as face-to-face • Still expensive to set up, but transmission costs are far cheaper • Technology has still not reached global industry standards and demands good infrastructure to be effective	• Depending on type of exchange, will have same ground rules as any other meeting for preparation, keeping focus, agreed signals for strong feelings, summarizing and followup • Will need to prioritize questions to avoid bothering others unnecessarily

TABLE 6 CONT'D
Global Team Technologies

TECHNOLOGY	ADVANTAGES	DISADVANTAGES	GROUND RULES
Virtual offices	• Meeting rooms, simultaneous desktop visual and data exchange • As close as you can get to sitting down in the same room with a group of people • May soon be able to split up the screen and focus in on people • You can move camera	• Expensive • Few standard, industry-tested, reliable products • Weak national infrastructures cannot support necessary data flow	• All the best practices and disciplines of other meetings still apply

Source: Adapted from Davison and Ward (1999).

TECHNOLOGY FOR BP GLOBAL TEAMS

BP's CEO, John Browne, has long recognized that the competitiveness of the global marketplace makes efficiency and innovation necessary for continuing success. Thus he has sought to help BP combine the agility of a small company with the resources of a large one. Browne quickly determined that one key element was to build the new BP through technology and global teams. In 1994 he launched the Global Virtual Teamwork Program in order to develop effective ways for members of teams to collaborate across different locations around the world. The project's primary aim was to let knowledgeable people talk to each other and then capture their expertise. BP wanted to build a network of people, not just a storehouse of data, information, or knowledge.

The software chosen for the Virtual Teamwork (VT) stations included desktop videoconferencing equipment, multimedia e-mail, application sharing, shared chalkboards, a document scanner, tools to record videoclips, groupware, and a web browser. The emphasis was on richness of

TECHNOLOGICAL SUPPORT AND COMMUNICATIONS

communication—on duplicating the nuances, variety, and human dimension of face-to-face contact.

A key early decision was that a newly created group would undertake the project. BP believed that the program would be less likely to fall into familiar information technology (IT) patterns if it were run by a group drawn from different parts of the company. Moreover, the absence of IT control would make it clear that the project was about communication, business change, and corporate behavior, not technology for its own sake.

The global teams were shown how to use the technology and learned how it could further their work. Team members communicated with each other using the VT stations—an ongoing real-life demonstration of the system's value as a tool for collaborative work and knowledge exchange. This kept the focus on the broad goal of encouraging project team members to discover untapped potential in themselves and the system. Only 20 percent of the technology coach's time was designated for showing the team how to use the system. The rest was devoted to helping team members link their business objectives to the system's capabilities and challenging them to consider the new ways of working that the VT system made possible (Davenport and Prusa, 1998).

There were numerous team successes. When equipment failure brought operations to a halt on a North Sea mobile drilling ship one day in 1995, for example, the ship's drilling engineers hauled the faulty hardware in front of a tiny video camera connected to one of BP's virtual teamwork stations. Using a satellite link, they dialed up the Aberdeen office of a drilling equipment expert who examined the malfunctioning part visually while talking to the shipboard engineers. He quickly diagnosed the problem and guided them through the necessary repairs. In the past, a shutdown of this kind would have necessitated flying an expert out by helicopter or sending the ships back to port and out of commission for several days (at $150,000 per day). This shutdown lasted only a few hours. Such a case demonstrates how virtual teamwork technology can get knowledge where it is needed. Technology had brought together the expert and the situation that required his expertise. His virtual presence gave shipboard engineers the benefit of his skill and experience, enabling them to understand the problem and solve it quickly.

Another example is the Andrew Project, a joint endeavor between BP, Brown & Root (a design and engineering firm based in Houston), and

Trafalgar House (a construction company based in Scotland) to build a new oil platform in the North Sea. Andrew team members took advantage of the application-sharing feature of the virtual team clients to write joint memos in ten or fifteen minutes that used to take hours or days by mail. Virtual meetings and virtual work sharing led to quantifiable benefits on the Andrew Project—including significant reductions in travel costs and expenses associated with bringing vendors on site. There were also measurable productivity improvements related to more efficient information searches and issue resolution, as well as reduction of duplication and wasted travel time. Virtual teamworking contributed significantly to the project's meeting its target date, to lower offshore costs, and to a much lower total cost of first oil—a key milestone in the development of a new field.

The technology did not eliminate the need for personal meetings, however. BP employees are still required to establish mutual trust and to hash out important issues involving large numbers of team members. Once they had met in person, though, participants found that videoconferencing maintained a sense of trust and direct personal contact that phone calls, e-mail, or memos could not provide. They discovered, for example, that participants were much more consistent with their commitments made via videoconferencing than those made via phone or mail.

Another important discovery was the value of "virtual coffee breaks" for global team members. These breaks consisted of people at up to eight different locations joining in video conversations with no set agenda. Just like American co-workers around the watercooler or Japanese R&D people in "talk rooms," the virtual team members discuss current work and describe problems they have been struggling with. These informal interactions often lead to explosions of creativity and successful project implementation (Davenport and Prusa, 1998).

USING COMMUNICATION AND DECISION-MAKING TECHNOLOGY

The use of electronic communication technologies is integral to the development of a high-performance global team. Global teams must learn how to capitalize on current technology for their long-distance work. Since these tools are changing so rapidly, a manager needs to keep learning about these tools and have the organization invest in the upgrade of equipment, software, and expertise (Sundstrom, 1999).

Implementing and managing communication technology is a difficult process that requires continuous monitoring and improvement. It's important to realize that there is a learning curve with any technology, and initial productivity may not indicate what lies ahead in the future. Be patient. When using technology for the first time, use it in a low-pressure situation—not in a critical project. Start with something easy.

First determine your business problem and business process. Then select and apply the appropriate technology to it. Don't purchase a collaboration tool without understanding the problems to be solved. Sometimes the best products have to be custom-made.

When implementing virtual meetings, it may be wise to use a facilitator to guide the meeting and make the transitions. (See Chapter 9 for the role of team facilitator.) If you are meeting in the same place, however, a team room with workstations and shared databases and storage areas helps to facilitate work. If you will be primarily communicating at different times through electronic sources, distributing members' photos and biographies will help to build trust. When using different vendors for different systems, make sure they have compatible software (Mittleman and Briggs, 1999; Sundstrom, 1999).

USING INFORMATION TECHNOLOGY

Gathering the most complete, comprehensive, and up-to-date information is essential for the development of an effective team. Teams need information not only to complete their work but also to develop new knowledge—a core product of many teams in today's economy (Bikson et al., 1999).

Teams should use a variety of task information, applications, and analytical tools. Teams also need to gather relevant data about their specific tasks. Software tools will enable them to extract new knowledge from this information:

> *Databases:* These systems are a "group memory that is shared and is used at least for formal information processing." In a corporation it

is a repository of data about business transactions, market forecasts, product descriptions, physical and human resources, and a host of other components. Computerized repositories, like databases, are the source of many, if not most, printed reports on business performance, past organizational behavior, and results of decisions (Hoffer and Valacich, 1993, p. 215).

World Wide Web: The web is an Internet application that allows file sharing. At its core is simply a file format called hypertext markup language (HTML) and a class of programs called browser that can read them. In most respects, it is just a text formatting language—except for two important differences. It allows the specification of links to other files (the hypertext capability) and allows file components to be multimedia in nature (graphics, audio/video, animation) (Marquardt and Kearsley, 1999).

Simulations: These computer-based programs can model actual equipment, processes, and activities.

Interactive and networked information technologies are essential for a global team. Responsive information systems allow team members to collect, monitor, and exchange information. When installing an information system, be sure to install an open-ended system that allows the team to modify it in a way that accommodates its work.

Team members, as well as anticipated users, must be involved in the design so that the proper information system is created. Team links should be created not only within the company and its databases but also with external databases relevant to team tasks such as customer data, training resources, and programming libraries. Special information systems may have to be designed to accommodate time-sensitive work (Bikson et al., 1999; Sundstrom, 1999).

THE INTERNET CREATES GLOBAL SUCCESS FOR GLOBAL TEAMS

As Marcia Stepanek (1999) noted in a recent issue of *Business Week,* more and more companies are showing that there's more to the World Wide Web than just cutting costs and speeding up communications. Today, increasing

TECHNOLOGICAL SUPPORT AND COMMUNICATIONS

numbers of companies are using global teams and the Internet to stimulate and manage innovation—and to put the brightest new ideas into the hands of the people who can turn them into products the most quickly.

The notion is that large companies can harness the web with small entrepreneurial global teams to drive innovation at a rate they have never before experienced. Hundreds of corporations are adopting this approach—from Nortel Networks to Procter & Gamble. DaimlerChrysler has created outposts of small global teams to scout around for new trends and products. A recent success at a Silicon Valley outpost is doing consumer research on electric cars and is helping designers in the early stages of Net-equipped automobiles. "The trend now is to decentralize operations, to build idea factories, or idea markets. This is a way to bring the start-up mentality inside," says Clayton Christensen, a Harvard Business School professor.

USING LEARNING TECHNOLOGIES

Companies all over the world are now investing in a wide variety of electronic learning technologies—that is, technologies that deliver information and facilitate the development of skills and knowledge. Computer delivery of training, use of Internet and network-based distance learning, electronic performance support systems (EPSS), and use of interactive/multimedia computer-based training are surging. Organizations now spend more than $4 billion a year on software for the intranet. Learning technology includes both presentation elements (how information is presented to learners) and distribution elements (how information is delivered to learners).

Presentation Technologies

- *Electronic text or publishing*—the dissemination of text via electronic means

- *Computer-based training (CBT)*—learning that uses computers to deliver training

- *Multimedia*—computer applications that use text, audio, animation, and video

- *Television*—one-way video combined with two-way audio or other electronic response systems

- *Teleconferencing*—the instantaneous exchange of audio, video, or text between two or more people or groups at two or more locations

- *Virtual reality*—a computer application that provides an interactive, immersive, and three-dimensional learning experience through fully functional, realistic models

- *EPSS*—an integrated computer application using expert systems, hypertext, embedded animation, and hypermedia to help users perform tasks

Distribution Technologies

- *Cable TV*—the transmission of television signals via cable technology

- *CD-ROM*—a format and system for recording, storing, and retrieving electronic information on a compact disc that is read using an optical drive

- *Electronic mail*—the exchange of messages through computers

- *Extranet*—a collaborative network that uses Internet technology to link organizations with their suppliers, customers, or other organizations sharing common goals or information

- *Internet*—a loose confederation of computer networks around the world that are connected through several primary networks

- *Intranet*—network within an organization

- *Local-area network (LAN)*—a network of computers sharing the resources of a single processor or server within a small geographic area

- *Wide-area network (WAN)*—a network of computers sharing the resources of one or more processors or servers over a large geographic area

TECHNOLOGICAL SUPPORT AND COMMUNICATIONS

- *Satellite TV (also called business TV)*—transmission of television signals via satellite

- *Simulator*—a device or system that replicates a real device or system

Global teams will be required to understand and use these learning technologies more and more as the team's need to learn while working becomes ever more commonplace—and ever more critical.

TECHNOLOGY: KEY FOR THE JAVABEANS GLOBAL TEAMS AT IBM

IBM is the world's top provider of computer hardware. With over 280,000 employees and annual sales approaching $100 billion, the company makes a broad range of computers, including PCs, notebooks, mainframes, and network servers. About 60 percent of the company's sales are to customers outside the United States. With a current focus on Internet business, IBM continues to revamp its image.

In 1997 IBM created a five-site, five-country global team that would work around the clock for the purpose of developing small components for the IBM VisualAge application. Rather than developing one large product release, IBM decided to develop many small components (known as beans) because each bean could be developed more rapidly. The new software components were to replace the immense software (called fatware) with smaller components, each of which would require less development time.

The original multisite project had four equal-size units of thirty-one professionals in four low-cost labor sites: Tsinghua University in Beijing; Bangalore, India; Minsk, Belarus; and Riga, Latvia. The group size of thirty-one was chosen because of past experiences with offshore sites. IBM managers concluded that they needed the right balance between a unit that is too small and not economically feasible in terms of setting up the infrastructure and one that is too large and unmanageable. In each site there were five core specialists in such areas as graphics and technical writing.

Part of the original vision was to create a team structure that could be used whenever IBM expanded its development to other sites around the world. This effort was originally envisioned in 1997 as a hub-and-spoke structure in which a strong centralized control group would reside in the

United States to initiate, review, allocate, and provide specialized services. At the outset the U.S. site consisted of a twenty-four-person unit in Seattle. The Seattle team played a dual role as both architects and users. Project management and other services were centralized in the Seattle site as well, including quality assurance and user interface specialists.

The project had a number of objectives. Building leading-edge technology (software components) while experimenting with a leading-edge management model to build the technology was important. JavaBeans are small components that are easier to define than large ones and for which development time is relatively short. This programming model would allow dispersed teams to design the beans and then work fairly independently from one another on each bean.

Another key goal for the global team was to pursue a "follow-the-sun" strategy that would lead to faster development of the product and shorter time to the customer. This goal proved hard to achieve on a continuous basis. From the outset, development was to be iterative. The product specification and the software product itself (the bean) were to go through many separate phases or iterations until complete. The U.S. command unit would set up a work specification for each JavaBean and assign it to an offshore site. The goal was to turn that spec into code by the end of the day and ship it back to Seattle for successive rounds of reviews and feedback. After reviewing and testing the code, the Seattle unit would specify changes and send instructions across the ocean for another iteration (Carmel, 1999).

IBM and the global teams faced a number of risks. IBM was simultaneously developing in five nations, with relatively inexperienced partners, and was doing it all with Java—a very young technology with an immature set of programming support tools.

INITIAL RESULTS

The daily turnaround was too ambitious for the offshore coders and U.S. reviewers alike. There was simply too much to digest in one day's work. Eventually the project was able to settle for two "code drops" from each remote site per week. In the meantime, the U.S. unit had assigned about half a dozen beans to each offshore site. So while Beijing sat waiting for a review and feedback on component 1, they worked on beans 2, 3, 4, 5, and 6. At steady state, the project was juggling about two dozen beans between the hub and the remote sites.

TECHNOLOGICAL SUPPORT AND COMMUNICATIONS

Shortly after the project and teams were initiated, a project manager was hired. He saw the entire project in a different light. A truly global development project, he said, should not be strongly centralized. Rather, it should resemble a network organization in which the various global partners coordinate activities among themselves rather than through a central unit. He also reasoned that having a large control center in the United States would defeat the primary purpose of a low-cost development project. The new manager changed the project into a network structure. The command unit was moved from Seattle to Raleigh where it was reduced to only three people—a global manager, a budget officer, and a chief technical architect—and thus became more of a project management unit responsible for oversight. The four offshore sites were now responsible for initiating projects.

This changed the development process. The U.S. hub's overall workload was reduced significantly, and responsibility for the tasks was passed to the foreign sites. In most cases, each bean's problem definition and coding was done by one of the four offshore sites. The symmetrical, phalanx structure was relaxed. The Minsk site became responsible for acceptance testing and integration for all beans (in addition to some of its own development). With responsibility devolving to the distant sites and the hub delegating tasks to these sites, the follow-the-sun strategy was no longer practical, although now and then there were certain time zone advantages.

WHY JAVABEANS GLOBAL TEAMS SUCCEEDED

The essence of making this complicated coordination process work was a strong collaborative technology infrastructure. All five sites were connected via local Internet providers to IBM's global network. The project director indicated that he could not manage such a complex process without ubiquitous collaborative technologies. The project was structured around a groupware server, IBM/Lotus Notes, which became the project's central repository, supporting special functions for structured communications such as issue management and action management. Other coordination activities centered on the Software Configuration Management system. Technology was properly deployed and used—and led to tremendous successes for IBM.

GUIDELINES FOR PROVIDING TECHNOLOGY TO GLOBAL TEAMS

Providing a technological infrastructure that allows for the collection of essential information, communicating, problem solving, and decision making across physical distances and time zones is a challenge that every global team must overcome if it is to be successful. The implementation of a technological infrastructure must be comprehensive and continually updated and reviewed. Here are some guidelines for designing and implementing a technological structure for global teams:

- Accentuate the *group* in groupware. Many of the human, cultural, and organizational challenges of global teams are more amenable to human sensitivity than to technical solutions.

- Although electronic communications may be acceptable in many situations, sometimes it's best to deliver "emotional" messages in person. (Videoconferencing and screen sharing may sometimes serve as acceptable substitutes.)

- Americans like to use rich communication media for tasks that require a rich message—that is, two-way interactions involving more than one sensory pattern (Carmel, 1999).

- When intensive problem solving, design, or conceptual collaboration needs to take place, global teams should choose the channel that allows for richest communication—for example, an airplane ride or videoconference. In general, important messages are best communicated through high-context means.

- The vision conveyed to participating cultures and groups must appeal to all emotional and motivational levels.

- Remember that the degree of rapport determines the context. Rich media convey more information and more emotion. Nonverbal communication is particularly important for high-context cultures.

- Team members may need to agree on a regular means of communication—whether via videoconference, voice mail, e-mail, fax, or a combination. If regular meetings are not possible due to time, distance, or expense, using multiple media helps create context. For example, a fax containing background information can help an overseas colleague prepare for a phone call—which can then be followed up by an e-mail to confirm major points.

TECHNOLOGY: THE ELECTRONIC ENABLER FOR GLOBAL TEAMS

Technology is a key component of the global team's infrastructure. Although technology assists in the development of an effective global team, it cannot create a successful team. It's no substitute for the human interactions that constitute the real core of global teamwork. As Devereaux and Johansen (1994, p. 141) note: "Links between human beings, not between machines, are the real challenge of globalization." Thus global teams must develop the human elements and their interactions to be effective. In Part IV we'll look at the HR alignments and human interactions essential for global teams.

Part Four

ALIGNING THE HUMAN RESOURCES

Chapter 8

Harnessing Cultural, Interpersonal, and Technical Expertise

When companies turn to teams to implement projects or specific tasks for the organization, they face a twin challenge. First they must find and appoint employees who have the background and potential to handle the tasks assigned to the team. But the company must also provide the training and resources necessary to enable those selected to acquire the knowledge, skills, and abilities needed to enhance their effectiveness to work with global teammates.

Because the team mode of working contrasts sharply with standard job descriptions, many organizations find that recruiting and developing employees for teams involves special selection and training issues. A growing number of companies—DuPont, Unilever, Siemens, GE, and Motorola, to name just a few—attribute the success of their global teams to the quality of members selected as well as the ongoing training, information, and support they are given. In this chapter we examine how Pfizer, a recent winner of the prestigious American Society for Training and Development (ASTD) award for "Global Team Development," harnessed the cultural, interpersonal, and technical expertise of its global teams.

PFIZER PHARMACEUTICALS AND GLOBAL TEAMS

Pfizer is a $11 billion global company with over 50,000 employees and 187 subsidiaries. Traditionally, Pfizer has operated as a "functionally siloed" organization with its country-specific business units operating within the walls of each of its country's borders. Recognizing the benefits of teams and given the silos and traditions of operating within country borders, Pfizer faced significant challenges in establishing and sustaining high-performing, global, cross-functional/cross-cultural teams.

A 1994 worldwide training audit revealed a growing need to train managers to work effectively with teams. As part of the corporate mission to increase its ability to operate globally, Pfizer sought to improve productivity and empower employees through the development of high-performance global teams. Although teams have been part of Pfizer's work processes for years, the company realized that, in many cases, these teams were in reality working groups that were falling short of operating at their highest potential—primarily because there was no system in place for selecting and developing high-performance teams.

Beginning in 1995, Pfizer's Pharmaceutical Development and Training Group (PD&T) began working with EquiPro International (a global consulting firm) for the purpose of creating a system for developing high-performance global teams. A key goal was to find ways to select and develop team members so that they could operate more effectively within the context of global teams. To create effective global teams, Pfizer realized that it had to

- Establish the structure and purpose of global teams within the context of the company's mission and vision
- Provide guidelines for selecting global team members and leaders
- Launch new global teams
- Identify stakeholders and their expectations of the teams
- Assess the effectiveness of currently functioning teams
- Establish metrics for measuring a team's effectiveness
- Develop team leaders' and members' roles and skills

CRITERIA FOR SELECTION

When organizations create a team or reorganize themselves around teams, they should recognize that their effectiveness depends on having employees with the right skills as well as a willingness to work effectively on a team (Klimoski and Zukin, 1999). This means thinking systematically about the criteria for selecting team members. They should be qualified in terms of experience and knowledge for the specific task assigned to the team as well as the interpersonal skills required to be an effective member of a team.

Although many selection criteria for single-nationality teams apply to global teams, the organization must recognize the special qualifications needed to select personnel from geographically and culturally different local units. What may be considered a "high-performance" characteristic at company headquarters, for example, may not apply to someone from a local country unit (Davison and Ward, 1999). Using standard headquarters criteria for "high performers" might weight the team selection process in a way that excludes representation from local units—and thus a team's ability to respond to local issues in a global organization (Snell et al., 1998).

Early in the team recruitment process, organizations should consider what characteristics to look for in potential team leaders and members. Here's an example of a set of competencies (what one global company calls "effectiveness criteria") for good team members:

- Universal standards for employees everywhere
- Ability to work within the culture and policies of the company
- Individual position capabilities
- Teamwork skills such as the ability to interact with others and negotiate (Klimoski and Zukin, 1999)

These competencies are just one way of looking systematically at what's needed for effective team performance. Another way is to determine broad attributes that will produce the desired outcomes. Glaxo-Wellcome, the global pharmaceutical firm, uses its own criteria for evaluating potential global project leaders.

SELECTING GLOBAL PROJECT MEMBERS AT GLAXO-WELLCOME

Glaxo-Wellcome looked for the following competencies and attributes for team members:

- Content awareness and curiosity (as opposed to content expertise)
- Tolerance of ambiguity
- Cultural awareness
- Results orientation
- Networking skills
- Ability to influence others
- Change leadership

It was important to select for these skills and attributes, as the company did not have a lot of time for development and training—although "just-in-time" development was incorporated into the team's face-to-face meetings. Local training and development professionals were also briefed on the needs of the team leaders. In turn, team leaders were encouraged to take advantage of any development opportunities that were offered locally and suited to their particular needs.

WHO DETERMINES THE SELECTION CRITERIA?

It's very important to guard against a cultural bias in deciding what makes a good team member. The characteristics selected should vary according to the type of team and the organization's style and culture. The responsibility for deciding on criteria usually falls to the HR group, who should work closely with the team's sponsoring unit or manager. The team leader then joins them in identifying the skills needed for various positions on the team. If the team is adding new members, the current members should participate in their selection.

If a company has no team leader positions prior to a reorganization, it could use focus groups to help develop criteria for choosing the global team leader. Senior managers who are team sponsors could be involved. One could also use other company criteria for team leaders as benchmarks. Whatever criteria an organization uses, the HR manager should know what training is likely to be needed and at what stage of staffing training should be used to reinforce the skills needed for a specific team.

Davison and Ward (1999) describe a company in which all managers were allowed to apply for a global project. They were given a case study to work on. An expert in global management rated the responses. The applicants were then interviewed about how they approached the different issues and why they reached certain conclusions. Through the exercise and the interviews, the company obtained information on how they would handle a situation, their ability to analyze, their use of strategic thinking in an ambiguous situation, and how they would deal with feedback.

Another company approached the selection criteria differently. Since its teams would be cross-functional and cross-geographical as well as work in the same place for several months, the criteria for selecting leaders were based on finding people who had been working across an entire business or geographic division. For team members, a list of criteria was sent to business units asking for nominations (examples: the best and brightest to reshape the company; language skills; people from a different region; those senior and available). From these lists the leadership made the final selection and allocated members to teams. There were two major advantages of this process: commitment to the criteria at the highest levels as well as the flexibility that local managers gained in choosing who to nominate. One disadvantage: Most team members and leaders were unsure why they had been selected—which meant that the team had to spend a lot of time clarifying their roles (Davison and Ward, 1999).

Typically leadership roles gravitate to people believed to have the most power and influence in the organization (or a particular group within the organization). The drawback to this selection method is that it limits the pool of successors to the current hierarchy, thus narrowing the potential pool of talent for team roles.

SELECTING MEMBERS FOR PFIZER'S GLOBAL TEAMS

Pfizer's European division embarked on a plan to establish three product teams that would be responsible for optimizing product performance through jointly developed sales, marketing, medical, manufacturing, registration, and public affairs initiatives. These Euroteams consisted of individuals from different countries and functions including medical, finance, sales, marketing, and information systems. Special efforts were made to select people who would work well in teams, who believed in Pfizer's global vision, and who brought expertise to the group.

The primary business challenge of the global teams was to maximize efficiency and creativity while leveraging resources across Europe. Soon after the Euroteams were formed, team members became aware of the need to establish effective relationships with their key stakeholder groups—which included senior management from each of the European countries as well as from product-specific teams in New York.

Moreover, the senior executives, managers, and professionals saw the need to improve competencies and experiences to ensure that the Pfizer teams could operate effectively in a global environment. There were also concerns about remote team management as many of the managers and leaders continued to live in their home countries while working on global teams. Pfizer clearly recognized that crossing borders of both national and functional interests and territories would require significant personal and organizational changes—and hence significant training and development.

TRAINING AND DEVELOPMENT

Participation in global teams calls for people with unique combinations of knowledge, skills, and abilities—as well as the potential to learn how attitudes and beliefs shape their view of people and business processes. Training and development should reinforce the assigned goals of the global team as well as its working style.

If the style of operation is to achieve local responsiveness, for example, training should develop capabilities in this area by giving members temporary assignments in a local unit. For conflict resolution and negotiation skills, training could be done outside the team sessions or before the team starts work. It should, however, be coupled with the actual work of having team members confront their differences in establishing ground rules for their work process (Snell et al., 1998).

Here are some guidelines for training a global team:

- Training content should be flexible so that members can learn and develop both individually and as a team.

- Training and the selection criteria for leaders and members of global teams should be aligned with the team's tasks and mission.

- Creating cross-cultural awareness and conflict resolution skills is an essential beginning. Language training can be a means of conveying awareness. Mock exercises or seminars attended by representatives from the countries where the global organization operates are other techniques that can be used.

- Training should aim at showing how teams achieve consensus. It should impact a thorough understanding of the team's mission and goals and how these relate to the organization's strategies, policies, and structures. This involves teaching skills in resolving misunderstandings and differing cultural views about style and methods of communication.

- Training should start before a team begins work, continue through the team's life cycle as needed, and end with the team telling the organization which methods helped or hindered achieving the team goal. This feedback can then be used for training future team leaders and members.

LANGUAGE AND GLOBAL TEAM DEVELOPMENT

Language differences are an obvious barrier to a team's integration and proficiency in solving problems. One English-French company initially pushed cross-language training on each side of the English Channel. After six months there was disillusionment on the British side about the short-term improvements they could expect from language training. The Paris office of the company—where personnel tended to have more English fluency than their English counterparts did in French—began an international management development seminar that utilized many of the techniques of training cross-cultural teams. The aim was to develop a better understanding of foreign language skills in presentation and negotiation.

The seminar produced a number of ideas on how to break through the language barrier. It was seen that language is not just a question of understanding words. Language conveys beliefs about the business process, for example, and can even be used to gain an advantage in negotiations. Gradually the executives at the seminar recognized that the conflicts about the use of language fit into a larger cultural and behavioral context. Bringing together company executives from different national and corporate cultures served a number of functions:

- To take a look at themselves in the mirror
- To ask others how they saw them
- To question others on the reasons for certain procedures or behavior
- To seek common ground for improving their own performance by aligning it with that of their foreign colleagues

As a result of the seminar, the company launched a successful senior executive program to build a new corporate identity.

The evolution of training in a German firm that had acquired a number of companies in the United States provides another model for cross-cultural training. Begun initially only for German executives transferring to U.S. assignments and Americans going to Germany, the training shifted to members of project teams that worked from offices in their respective countries. The training consisted of five ascending levels of courses: language, cultural awareness, intercultural communication, interaction workshops, and on-site consulting with key project leaders and project teams. Trainees entered the program where it fit their level of knowledge, experience, and skill.

In the interaction workshops, lasting three days, six Americans and six Germans learn about the differences in their work styles, attitudes, and communication—and then seek solutions to breakdowns and misunderstanding. The methods include simulating business meetings and analyzing videorecordings of work in single-culture and bicultural groups.

HARNESSING EXPERTISE

TAILORING THE TRAINING TO THE GLOBAL TEAM'S CULTURES

In looking for models of cross-cultural training, organizations can find a wide range of content and presentation styles. The objective is to meet a team's particular development needs—taking into account cultural preferences, learning styles, and the availability and sophistication of training resources. Training can be done throughout the company as a preparation for cross-cultural interaction. This develops a core of team leaders. Training can also be done for a specific team. It can take place where the actual team works—that is, off the job or on the job. When teams are intact and functioning, they can receive "just-in-time" training as the need arises while they work (Davison and Ward, 1999).

The process of creating new materials or adapting materials for use in other cultures is not a simple task. The trainers must not only translate the materials but carefully transpose them for a totally new environment in a way that gains acceptance in the local culture. Those involved in developing global teams should assume cultural differences rather than similarities. They should treat each cultural environment as requiring culturally appropriate training materials that will not be resisted by learners.

There are a number of culturally specific guidelines to consider as you develop training materials:

- Avoid culturally inappropriate pictures or scenarios—such as scantily clad women in Arab cultures.

- Use plenty of graphics, visuals, and demonstrations if the trainees are learning in a second language.

- Provide lots of handouts and instructional materials—these are highly valued and even displayed in many cultures.

- Beware of corporate ethnocentrism demanding that the company must be presented exactly the same all over the world.

As global teamwork becomes more prevalent, simply training today's leaders and members is not sufficient. Developing the next generation is an important part of succession planning. There are several ways of developing future team leaders: give them overseas experience; assign them as team members; have them interview actual team leaders; and ask them to become the facilitator of a team.

DEVELOPMENT AND TRAINING FOR PFIZER TEAMS

Pfizer assembled a group of both internal and external training/OD consultants along with a representative group of country executives, team leaders, and team members. This planning group devoted six months to analyzing how Pfizer's global teams were performing. They concluded that the global team's structure and processes were due for a major overhaul.

The group recommended that Pfizer provide training for people serving on global teams. This training would be piloted by a headquarters team with cross-functional/cross-cultural representation. The group also recognized that the role of senior executives and key stakeholders had to be assessed since a true culture change would require their support. Senior management would need to provide resources and eliminate political and cultural obstacles for the global teams. Thus the group determined that key senior executives and other stakeholders must be involved in the early stages of the formation of global teams.

A workshop called "Crossing the Borders" was developed for new teams. Its purpose was to help the global team develop a common language and a blueprint for success. During these workshops, a new team works together to develop its charter, boundaries, values, and operating principles, its stakeholder and operating practices, and its cross-functional/cross-cultural teamwork roles and skills. The two-day development program enables participants to:

- Understand the importance of cross-functional teamwork for achieving the company's mission and vision
- Recognize the stages and process of team development
- Understand—and use—the roles of team leaders, team facilitators, and team members
- Receive individual and team survey feedback on strengths and weaknesses
- Develop a set of team values

- Develop a team mission and vision, including team goals
- Understand the importance of team tasks and sensitive issues
- Understand the critical factors that contribute to team success or failure
- Prioritize the critical skills required for team effectiveness
- Develop action plans for building individual and team skills

The program uses a variety of training methodologies—ranging from surveys and small-group discussions to a case study, team activities, and other experiential learning activities customized to the program's learning objectives.

The team development system, which began with just three European teams, has proved so successful that the number of global teams around the world has quadrupled in just one year with the proactive support of senior management. The Pfizer global training team has attained the following results:

- To date, 500 executives, managers, professionals, and administrative staff have received training. In 1998, Pfizer extended its use of technology-based (groupware) interventions to expand training and support to more staff worldwide.
- There has been improved management of team meetings through the use of preliminary agendas, the appointment and use of facilitators and timekeepers, and the institution of explicit decision-making processes.
- More clearly defined roles, responsibilities, levels of empowerment, explicit operating expectations, and agreements now exist among team members and key stakeholders.
- Goal setting and prioritization have been aligned with budgets and individual performance objectives.

As noted in the award given to Pfizer by the American Society for Training and Development, a number of guidelines emerged from the company's experience with global teams:

- Above all, there must be a business or performance challenge that is best addressed by a global team.

- Global teams must receive training and development in teamwork skills such as communications, problem solving, decision making, and facilitation.
- There should be a strong commitment by all key stakeholder groups to support the global teams and to develop mutual expectations and measures of success. Senior executives must demonstrate their support and commitment to the team.
- Global teams need a clear charter and set of boundaries.
- Key stakeholders need to participate in and support the global team's charter and boundaries as well as the team's project and budgets.
- Global teams must develop their own internal roles, operating agreements, and guidelines for border management with key stakeholders.
- The country management/functional bosses of individual team members must be committed to honoring and supporting members' roles and responsibilities.
- The organization should provide appropriate rewards or recognition for the global team as a whole as well as for individual members.
- Global team members must be able to balance their personal and team roles and their professional development opportunities.
- There should be significant investment in team development.
- Global teams must stay focused on achieving goals that are directly tied to the business results which align members' accountability.
- Territorial or silo cultures threaten the viability of global teams.

Since piloting the system, Pfizer has created high-performing Euroteams to work on product issues that span Europe. Pfizer also has launched twenty new global teams in Canada, Latin America, Asia, Europe, and Africa/Middle East, with plans under way to establish a Center of Excellence for Global Teams to expand the company's internal consulting resources. Pfizer is using the system to find new ways to cross-pollinate and leverage resources across country borders and organizational functions. As a result of the effectiveness of its well-selected and well-trained global teams, Pfizer is changing its infrastructure and its institutional culture as well as creating global success.

HARNESSING EXPERTISE

SUSTAINING THE SYNERGY

Global teams generally have more talent and potential than other types of teams. Yet this potential is often squandered because of the organization's and team's inability to harness the power. HR policies that optimize the selection and development of these people as well as the entire group can increase rather than diminish the team's potential. To sustain and enhance these capabilities, global teams should have skilled facilitation and be able to measure and reward performance—issues we will tackle in the next three chapters.

Chapter 9

Global Team Facilitators

As we observed in Chapter 3, all global teams need effective leadership to manage and administer the group's activities and tasks. But many global teams are discovering that they also need a facilitator to guide and manage the dynamics—and avoid the possible chaos—of teams composed of multicultural members separated by time and distance.

Many of us now see a high payoff in having a person whose role is to keep the global team on track and help it work through the complex interactions. As Ward (1999, p. 18) notes, if global facilitators work effectively with the global team throughout its life cycle, they can "ensure that the strategic moments experienced by the team are crafted into performance enhancing experiences and do not destroy the team's ability to function effectively."

Sue Davison (1996) writes that one company calculated the daily cost of its global team at $150,000—and the daily profit from its best-selling product at up to $3 million! If an external facilitator can genuinely smooth and speed the work process, even by a few days, how much might this person be worth?

WHY GLOBAL LEADERS NEED A FACILITATOR

Often we point to the team leader for guidance. Team leaders, however, have their hands full with managing and administering the activities and tasks of the group. More important, a leader is usually right in the middle of the action—a position that doesn't usually offer a holistic perspective. It's difficult to understand conflict or communication issues when you are part of the process (and indeed may be part of the problem). It is analogous to CEOs providing management consultation to their own organizations. An outside perspective is needed—especially one that can provide a holistic understanding of the dynamic and complex interactions among team members.

Eventually a global team will realize that it needs a facilitator to provide insight and guidance to the dynamic processes of its multicultural (and possibly dispersed) members. Succinctly, a facilitator's sole role is to keep the global team on track and work out the complex interactions of its members. This role involves coaching team leaders and members on how to work more effectively together and with the organization they serve. What's more, the facilitator helps members develop skills they will need both as individuals and as members of a team (Davison and Ward, 1999).

In this chapter we explore three key aspects of a global team facilitator: the facilitator's role, values, functions, and characteristics; the facilitation components that are unique and challenging in a global team; and the techniques that are particularly useful in facilitating and coaching global teams. Throughout the chapter we will illustrate in a facilitator's own words how she worked with a global team. We'll also see how General Motors used facilitation to improve the work of its global teams.

FACILITATION OF A GLOBAL PHARMACEUTICAL COMPANY

Isabel Rimanoczy

In 1996, a European-headquartered multinational pharmaceutical company divided its operations into regions. The regional manager for Latin America, facing the challenge of developing synergy among the managers in his region, gathered key people for the purpose of launching a new product and creating a cross-functional regional team. The challenge was not easy.

Although Latin America is, with the exception of Brazil, a Spanish-speaking region, there are still significant cultural differences that are not always obvious.

The regional team included executives from Argentina, Brazil, Chile, Colombia, Ecuador, Mexico, Uruguay, and Venezuela. They were scheduled to hold five one-day meetings, spread over six months, hosted in different countries of the region. Establishing a successful project and team were deemed important for several reasons:

- From the business side, the launching of the new product was a key factor in facing competitors.
- From an organizational point of view, the success of this mission meant a message for the whole region—and for the other regions in the world: Synergy makes sense.
- From a team perspective, the fact that a cross-functional and cross-cultural team could perform with success would be seen as a role model for other projects.
- From a personal point of view, the CEO and group members were taking a chance with an audacious project.

After the group's second meeting, the CEO, aware of the importance of this pilot test of regional synergy, decided to call in a facilitator/learning coach to help the team in its subsequent meetings. This gave the global team a chance to further transform their project into a learning experience. As learning coach, I began by making personal contact with every member before the next meeting in order to explain the facilitation approach I would be employing for the rest of the meetings.

THE TEAM FACILITATOR'S ROLES, VALUES, AND FUNCTIONS

The team facilitator can be a critical factor for the success of any team. Their values and the manner in which they perform their functions can quickly move a team toward achieving both short-term and long-term goals. Let's now examine those roles, values, and functions.

Roles

Facilitation has become a crucial ingredient in organizations undergoing change—whether they are developing new products and services, empowering employees, developing shared visions, or instilling self-management for work teams. Group facilitation has been defined as follows: "a process in which a person who is acceptable to all members of the group, substantively neutral, and has no decision-making authority intervenes to help a group improve the way it identifies and solves problems and makes decisions, in order to increase the group's effectiveness" (Schwarz, 1994, p. 4).

It is precisely because groups find it difficult to look at their behavior that they need a facilitator. The facilitator helps the group improve its internal dynamics and processes: how members address each other, how they make decisions, how they give and understand information, how they manage conflict and differences (Schwarz, 1994).

Ideally, a facilitator should be involved both in the start-up and initial meeting stages and throughout the team process (Davison and Ward, 1999). The facilitator's approach requires sincere dedication to certain values about human relations and team functioning. This role can only be accomplished if the facilitation is well timed—both in its duration and in the point of entry.

Thus, as we can see, global facilitation is not a one-time process; it needs to be ongoing. Time and time again, global teams have found that if they have a facilitator working with them throughout their life cycle, they can become confident in handling critical issues.

In too many instances, the need for a facilitator is recognized too late—after a global team is already formed and has run into trouble. If the problems of team functioning, particularly those that are complicated by cross-cultural members, are not addressed in the early stages of the team's life cycle, the chances of the team achieving its goals are greatly reduced. And the cost of the team effort, prolonged by stalemate or unresolved conflict, is greatly increased (Davison and Ward, 1999).

Global teams cannot afford to wait for such serious problems to surface before bringing in a facilitator. Yet companies—unsure of the payoffs compared to the costs—are often reluctant to call in a facilitator. One facilitation consultant notes: "Companies will spend millions on making computer and information systems across the globe compatible, but are reluctant to invest a fraction of that in facilitating teams to work together" (Young, 1998b, p. 51). Once the need for a facilitator is recognized, however, the limits of this person's role must be carefully defined.

Values

A facilitator is a guide, not a director. The facilitator does not tell team members how to do their job. The facilitator's job is to make it *easier* for them to do their job. Certain values concerning personal relationships and individual action guide this work. Schwarz (1994) cites three values that are indispensable for the effective facilitator.

- *Free and informed choices.* This means that team members will be able to define their objectives and find specific methods to achieve them. These choices are made with valid information. Thus facilitators do not make decisions for people; they provide accurate information to help people decide if they want to change their behavior.

- *Valid information.* Team members share all relevant information in a way that people can understand and validate. They are constantly collecting more information to determine if they should change their decisions.

- *Internal commitment to the choice.* People feel responsible for the decisions they make. They make these choices not because they will be rewarded or penalized but because they find them compelling and satisfying.

All of these values are related to one another. People use valid information to make an informed choice. When they make these free and informed choices, they are then committed to them. When they are committed to their decisions, they take responsibility to see that they are implemented. The job of the facilitator, then, is to help groups act in ways consistent with these assumptions (Schwarz, 1994).

Functions

What are the main functions of the global team facilitator? This question can be answered by ruling out certain functions—such as voting, assuming decision-making power, acting as a go-between for the group and its sponsor, and arbitrating disputes. Rather, the facilitator's job is twofold: (1) helping the team process to get the assigned task done and (2) helping the team to build a capacity for self-management of its work process (Schwarz, 1994; Wageman, 1997).

The facilitator is like a mechanic who not only fixes the team's vehicle well enough to arrive at its destination but teaches the members how to maintain, repair, and redesign the vehicle so it will reach any desired destination (Schwarz, 1994). In both cases, facilitators bring certain unique contributions to the group process:

- They note what people do and say, and they identify similarities, differences, and synthesis of the positions expressed.
- They intervene when they see ineffective behavior.
- They conduct themselves as role models for behavior on the team.
- They give the team positive feedback (Schwarz, 1994; Berger, 1996a).

When facilitators seek to build a team's self-management capacity, they perform two additional functions: (1) providing rewards when the team is managing itself effectively and (2) teaching the team how to use problem-solving processes (Wageman, 1997).

UNIQUE FEATURES OF FACILITATION

Global teams face unique hurdles that make the facilitator's role particularly useful in helping members to learn what makes the difference between success and failure and discover what team members have in common in order to minimize the difficulties of team meetings and personal interactions. Facilitators can help teams overcome difficulties in three areas (Davison and Ward, 1999; Berger, 1996a):

- Differences in members' cultural norms relating to such factors as how their cultural background influences their expectations about team goals and processes, leadership styles, and their individual status on the team
- Degree of fluency in the team's common language
- National composition and geographic spread of the team

GLOBAL TEAM FACILITATORS

The challenge for facilitators is to help the team recognize and confront these barriers as soon as possible. They continue by helping the team to see how conflicts over procedures are influenced by these barriers.

The facilitator's job depends on the phase of the global team's work. The start-up phase is perhaps the most crucial, for this is when cultural and organizational issues have the maximum power to create tensions. The time invested at this phase pays off in the following stages of the team's life. Again, the slogan "start slow, end fast" is a good guide.

The facilitator should work with the sponsors on the team's composition and point out the cultural factors that will influence how they perform. Interviewing key members or surveying all members about their expectations, how they would like the team to function, and where problems could arise in the process are important issues for the facilitator to explore early in the life of the global team (Davison and Ward, 1999).

In the start-up phase the facilitator also needs to find out the reasons for the team's makeup (diversity of skills, similarity of jobs performed in the organization, political considerations) and each member's level of commitment to the team. In the initial meetings, the facilitator should:

- Ensure that different expectations of team members are brought to the surface and aired so that the team can work more effectively. This can be done through brainstorming, prioritizing, and goal-setting exercises. One method is to have different members role-play the style of a member from a different culture. Americans, for example, who generally are action-oriented, may find it difficult to work with members from cultures that value social interaction more highly than quick results.

- Work on building face-to-face relationships. This may require not only discussion by the team as a whole or individually with each other but also scheduling social activities that promote these relationships.

- Establish how team members will give each other feedback. This can help overcome cultural expectations that inhibit feedback or make certain feedback styles unacceptable. Try using appropriate cultural approaches (Hofstede, 1991; Trompenaars, 1994). These can be used to create flip charts or other visuals that highlight the values applicable to a particular team.

- Identify how time-zone differences and means of communication (e-mail, videoconferences) can be managed to maintain interaction between meetings.

In the ongoing stages of the global team's activities, the facilitator needs to assist the leader in making sure that team involvement is maintained as deadlines loom (as opposed to relying solely on a core group or the headquarters representatives). Given that cultural differences cause some members to speak up more than others, the facilitator and leader should be sensitive to differences in language fluency and cultural views of status on the team. By making detailed observations or playing videotapes of sessions, the facilitator can bring out the degree to which some members are being excluded—or others are dominating the process.

The facilitator should use the time between group meetings for reviewing how the process is going. Make sure that the team process is documented by questionnaires and checklists that can be used in evaluating team performance at the end. Gradually, the facilitator can reduce his presence in meetings as the team and leader become more proficient in the process. In fact, skillful process facilitators may gradually work themselves out of a job.

SKILLS OF THE SUCCESSFUL GLOBAL FACILITATOR

Since a major responsibility is to assist the team in its interactions, the facilitator must be able to see, understand, and then reflect that process to the team. A team facilitator must therefore possess skills in diagnosis, interpretation, and reflection:

Diagnosis skills: the ability to keep quiet, avoid putting words in the mouth of others, hear what is said (as well as not said), and ask exceptionally good questions—questions that make people think but, at the same time, make them feel challenged and supported rather than criticized

Interpretation skills: the ability to stand apart from the action in order to bring to the surface the process issues; to understand group processes; to tolerate ambiguity

Reflection skills: the ability to provide feedback; willingness to confront; good judgment as to when to direct the group's attention away from the task to the learning; quality of openness, frankness, patience, empathy; skill in timing feedback—too early and the intervention is not understood, too late and the opportunity has passed

In a global team environment a facilitator must have specific skills concerning cultural awareness and sensitivity. Global and cross-cultural experts have cited ten key competencies essential for people who wish to be effective in global facilitation assignments (Marquardt and Engel, 1993). Let's look at these ten skills in detail.

Knowledge of One's Own Culture

"Know thyself" is the most important intercultural skill of global professionals. Our behavior is obviously influenced by our cultural values, beliefs, and assumptions. Unless we become conscious of these values and examine them carefully, we won't understand why we act the way we do—and react toward other cultures the way we do.

Knowledge and Appreciation of Other Cultures

Global facilitation requires that one understand key elements of the culture:

- Religious beliefs and process
- Family and social structure
- Educational system
- Politics and government
- Historical and cultural achievements
- Economics and industry
- Geographic and demographic information
- Sports, entertainment, and symbols

Having such information will provide reference points, case studies, resources, and so forth. This makes the facilitation professional more relevant and demonstrates interest in the local people.

Global Perspective and Mind-Set

People with a global mind-set have the ability to expand their knowledge continually. Such people have a highly developed conceptual capacity to deal with the complexity of global organizations. They are extremely flexible, strive to be sensitive to cultural diversity, are able to intuit decisions with less-than-perfect information, and have a strong capacity for reflection.

A global mind-set sees the world globally, is open to exchanging ideas across borders, is able to break down provincial ways of thinking. Here the emphasis is on balancing global and local needs—and being able to operate cross-functionally, cross-divisionally, and cross-culturally around the world.

Respect for the Values and Practices of Other Cultures

Most Americans grow up believing that their way is the best way of thinking and behaving; to think or act otherwise would be foolish. Our mind is programmed to think in a certain way. Society—through religion, schools, politics, and other cultural factors—reinforces this ethnocentric way of acting. Americans in particular have been taught not only that their way is best but that other ways are inferior and need to be changed.

So it's hard to accept that other ways of thinking should be respected. Global facilitators must appreciate other cultures—not that other cultures are better or worse than ours, but simply different. It is exactly this nonjudgmental attitude that is so critical for effective global activities. Team members of other cultures will easily recognize whether their way of life is respected by you or rejected.

Facilitators must be able to grasp what the other culture considers important as well as how organizations and individuals function in the cultural context. Unfamiliar perspectives and behavior should be examined in the context of the culture. The ability to suspend judgment temporarily, recognize the possible validity of a differing perspective, and find a way of building together is one of the biggest challenges facing the global facilitator.

Cultural Flexibility

Most Americans begin a global assignment with excitement. But sooner or later, this euphoria is followed by confusion, frustration, and psychological disorientation caused by the new culture and environment. Coping with the unavoidable stress of a cross-cultural setting is difficult.

Yet patience and tolerance of ambiguity are a critical component for working and living abroad. The ability to react to new and even unpredictable situations with little apparent discomfort is very important for anyone working overseas. Flexibility and emotional resilience are traits that expand your range of options so that you're able to deal effectively with different situations.

Ability to Acculturate the Interventions

Acculturation is necessary to convey the facilitation efforts across cultural boundaries—or, to use a computer term, to ensure that the training program is user-friendly. Acculturated facilitation eliminates as many roadblocks to the team as possible. The global facilitator's objective is to ensure, not only that improved interactions occur, but also that the interactions are appropriate for the cultural milieu. Without this acculturation, there will be much less learning and much less change.

Communication Skills

Listening and speaking are much more complex in cross-cultural settings—yet much more important. Understanding nonverbal as well as verbal messages requires a high level of communication skills including the ability to ask open-ended questions, to be silent, to paraphrase, and to reflect feelings. In some cultures, we may not even be able to ask questions to verify what we are experiencing since inquisitiveness may be perceived as inappropriate or even rude.

More and more global facilitators are stressing the importance of speaking—or at least understanding—basic phrases as well as the structural content of the native language. Language is important because it reflects cultural nuances: Mandarin suggests a sense of hierarchy, place, and order; the Thai language shows great respect for elders; the Spanish language reflects a passive locus of control. In addition to the spoken language, nonverbal language is critical too in understanding a culture. The body language, gestures, and environment of a high-contact culture often speak more clearly and completely than the verbal language.

Cultural Empathy

Global facilitators must attend to other cultures. Through context and nonverbal behavior—rather than questions that are too personal, embarrassing, or probing for the culture—they must be able to understand what is happening and what is expected. Establishing personal relationships is critical for facilitation's effectiveness in most cultures, and this takes time and effort.

Most facilitation work involves the gathering and utilization of information. This is difficult enough in one's own culture, but it's even more challenging in a different culture where the possibility of error is magnified. It is vital to be able to gather information and make sure that one's own cultural biases don't affect its accuracy or interpretation. The successful global facilitator can blend two or more cultural perspectives and interpret them in a way that transcends them all.

Patience and Sense of Humor

Adapting to a different environment calls for tremendous patience. That we can control time and the future is a fundamental American belief—but one that may be totally opposite to the beliefs of other cultures. Though waiting for consensus is extremely difficult for Americans, it's essential in working throughout the world.

A sense of humor as one deals with the unexpected and the unknown is surely needed in cross-cultural situations. Stress can be very acute in global situations where you don't know what to expect and may be totally surprised by someone's behavior. A sense of humor is indispensable for dealing with the cultural mistakes every global facilitator is certain to commit.

Commitment to Continuous Learning

Globalization has made change ever faster and ever more chaotic. Technology and the worldwide explosion of information have increased the expectation that the global facilitator must learn not only continuously but more quickly and with greater focus. Solutions that worked in one's own culture may be impractical or totally inappropriate in another culture. Problem solving with people of other cultures calls for new approaches, since participative approaches and brainstorming may not be culturally accepted. Worksheet 4 provides a checklist where you can evaluate your skills for effective global team facilitation and decide on appropriate developmental activities.

GLOBAL TEAM FACILITATORS

WORKSHEET 4

Assessing the Global Team Facilitator's Competencies

Directions: Next to each of the competencies indicate your assessment of your comfort and skill. ("Comfort" and "skill" are defined below.) Use a circle to indicate your self-rating on each of the items. After you have finished your assessment add up your total comfort score, your total skill score, and your overall competency score. The scoring key is located at the end of the assessment.

- *Comfort:* How easily can you perform this competency? Does this competency fit your style and image?
- *Skill:* Are you skilled in performing this competency?

COMPETENCIES	COMFORT				SKILL				TOTAL
	None	Low	Medium	High	None	Low	Medium	High	
1. Knowledge of your own culture	1	2	3	4	1	2	3	4	
2. Knowledge and appreciation of other cultures	1	2	3	4	1	2	3	4	
3. Global perspective and mind-set	1	2	3	4	1	2	3	4	
4. Respect for the values and practices of other cultures	1	2	3	4	1	2	3	4	
5. Cultural flexibility	1	2	3	4	1	2	3	4	
6. Ability to acculturate interventions	1	2	3	4	1	2	3	4	
7. Communication skills	1	2	3	4	1	2	3	4	
8. Cultural empathy	1	2	3	4	1	2	3	4	

GLOBAL TEAMS

WORKSHEET 4 CONT'D

Assessing the Global Team Facilitator's Competencies

COMPETENCIES	COMFORT				SKILL				TOTAL
	None	Low	Medium	High	None	Low	Medium	High	
9. Patience and sense of humor	1	2	3	4	1	2	3	4	
10. Commitment to continuous learning	1	2	3	4	1	2	3	4	
Total									

Scoring Key

Add up the circled numbers and write your total score below. The following chart interprets your score and suggests corrective action.

Total score: _____

Score	20–40	41–60	61–80
Interpretation	Lack of facilitation and comfort	Somewhat effective comfort and skill	Very comfortable and skillful
Action	You need to find a context in which you can develop your skill and comfort levels. This includes finding places to experience and experiment with facilitation, taking courses in team facilitation, and possibly working with a skilled facilitator in order to gain feedback and a role model.	You are somewhat effective and need to build on your comfort or skill level. Find places where you can receive direct feedback on your expertise—either in a course or in the field. This type of reflection will allow you to target your work and competency development.	You feel very comfortable and skillful in global facilitation. You will probably want to build on your repertoire of skills by putting yourself in a variety of facilitation contexts including different industries and with different levels of employees.

GLOBAL TEAM FACILITATORS

GUIDELINES FOR FACILITATION

For the organization sponsoring a global team, there are certain preliminary guidelines for using facilitation: It must be incorporated from the start of the team design and the initial stages of teamwork; sufficient resources and time must be allowed for it to become part of the team process; and in selecting facilitators the organization should take into account the cultural composition of the teams they will be working with. Relying solely on a headquarters facilitator or one from a local unit abroad may create problems. In some cases, using a team of facilitators from business units viewed as having lower status in the organization may make members from those units more comfortable with the facilitation process.

Once a facilitator has been selected, the basic guidelines for their effective functioning in global teams can be grouped into five areas. The first is *values*. The facilitator does not tell team members how to do their job—the task is to make it easier for them to do their job by giving them information about effective personal and group interaction. The team then has the choice whether or not to use this knowledge.

The second area is *strategizing*. Facilitators should recognize they have different roles at various stages of the team's life cycle—concentrating efforts at the design and initial stages and gradually turning over management of process to the team leadership and members as they become more competent.

The third area is *dealing with cultural diversity*. This means building consensus about how to surmount cultural differences and perceptions of team objectives, processes, leadership style, and status of individual members. Though "book knowledge" of these differences is useful, team members must recognize their presence and experience their effect on *their* group's performance. Discussion, role playing, use of cross-cultural visual "maps," utilizing data supplied by team members, using feedback about shared values and outlooks—all are useful techniques for accomplishing this. The facilitator's own ways of responding to cultural differences and giving members feedback on their participation can also serve as a role model in this regard. Scheduling sufficient social time for team members to become acquainted with each other is also advisable.

Fourth is *communication*. Aside from fostering positive verbal interactions, the facilitator should encourage the team to reach consensus on how to accommodate differing degrees of fluency (spoken and written) in the team's common language. These decisions should take into account communication difficulties when the team is not meeting face-to-face—such as differing time zones and limited access to telephone, e-mail, and videoconferencing.

Fifth is *capturing lessons learned*. As observers free from the responsibility of participating in the substantive work of the group, facilitators should use their time to document problems that arise in the team process. These can then be presented to the team for discussion. At the end of the process, the facilitator should encourage team members to summarize the lessons learned—and to communicate these lessons to the sponsoring organization for use in the future.

Facilitators should be sure to introduce themselves and their role in a clear and supportive way. Their work must not be seen as threatening or causing loss of face. They should pose questions to the group as a whole—rather than toward individuals—and demonstrate the value of sharing the learning. Facilitators must create an environment that encourages asking questions and challenging the status quo. They should be comfortable with periods of silence (an Asian custom) or outbursts of expression (Hispanic and Arabic), appreciate indirectness and formality, and understand nonverbal communication patterns and context.

AN INSIDE LOOK AT FACILITATION

Isabel Rimanoczy

The facilitator pays special attention to the way the group is acting. She intervenes when the process becomes an obstacle to the group making progress on the content. A key objective is to create moments of reflection so that members of the group have a chance to review their acts, draw conclusions, and make the required changes to ensure better progress on the task. The facilitator is a "connector" in this process—designing, observing, questioning, teaching, and coaching—with a just-in-time approach to intervention.

ACTION/REFLECTION LEARNING CYCLE
- Phase 1: Action
- Phase 2: Reflection

- Phase 3: Awareness
- Phase 4: Assessing the need for change
- Phase 5: Planning
- Phase 6: New action
- Throughout: Planning by learning

As the facilitator and learning coach, my role during the sessions was to:

- Provide tools or concepts if they could help in working more efficiently.
- Stop the team to ask a question that would help them reflect on their current performance.
- Help the team recognize the learning occurring during the session.
- Help in creating the link between that situation and others they would face daily when working on other teams.
- Help them stay focused on the task.
- Provide feedback upon request.

Two key moments of truth emerged during the sessions when significant change and learning occurred.

INTERVENTION 1

At one point I invited the group to suggest one or two norms they considered essential to ensuring a good performance during the meeting (Phases 1 and 2: Action and Reflection). One of the norms that arose was "to use English," the official language of the meetings, although English is not the native language of any of the countries of the region. This provoked the sudden awareness (Phase 3) of the following:

- In this company, if you want a good career you must speak good English.
- These meetings were being held in English because they were meetings of people wanting a good career in the organization.
- Some hierarchical attendants would assess the participants according to their English skills.
- English is a learned language, and nobody felt entirely comfortable speaking English.

- Some people may prefer not to express an idea rather than expose their imperfect English.

Immediately after this, I asked the group if English was an obstacle to communication and if the group accepted that norm (Phase 4: assessing the need for change). Members agreed that it did—and, with obvious relief, decided that everyone was free to speak whichever language they preferred (Phase 5: planning). The meeting continued in Spanish (Phase 6: new action).

This event shows how a taboo topic in the organization (namely, the importance of English) was hindering the group's communication, one of the difficulties they had diagnosed. As the learning coach, I highlighted how the fact of setting norms had helped the team in their performance, fostering their awareness of learning to be repeated in other situations.

INTERVENTION 2

Their meeting had a tight agenda with presentations every thirty minutes run by different members who explained the progress they were making in launching the product. They used overheads and charts to explain the data. They inspired some questions, but the tight time schedule didn't allow for many questions or much discussion. Even so, after the third presenter they were already fifty minutes behind schedule. Everyone began to worry since the group needed to finalize everything by the end of the session.

At this point (Phase 1: action) I suggested a "stop—reflect—write—report," which is a tool used to include a moment of reflection (Phase 2) immediately after an action. I suggested two questions: What are we doing well, and what should we be doing differently? The group had two minutes to write down their thoughts individually. Then everyone would read aloud their two answers. As a result of this intervention, we collected a number of "awareness" thoughts (Phase 3), including:

- The time schedule is not being respected.
- There is no time to ask questions.
- There is no time for major exchanges.
- The data presented in overheads is merely one-way communication.
- The time of the meeting should be used better.

GLOBAL TEAM FACILITATORS

The group then moved to Phase 4 (assessing the need for change) to determine how they might improve their teamwork. They concluded that a meeting of so many people from different countries was a unique opportunity for a face-to-face exchange and should be used more wisely. Everything that could be handled by e-mail, fax, or phone should be avoided at these sessions, thus saving the meeting for questions, generation of ideas, and exchange of experiences.

Getting information was still important, however, so they decided to review the priorities to be discussed during the rest of that day. The remaining presentations were rescheduled for a future meeting as well as what additional information needed to be distributed to each member (Phase 5: planning). The learning went one step further (Phase 6: new action) as they planned what information they would mail prior to their next meeting to prevent the same thing from happening again.

LESSONS

Above all, I have realized the critical importance of beginning with a question: "What are we here for?" As simple as it may seem, once a group takes a moment to reflect on this question, the whole work is easily focused. If the Latin American group had begun with that question (answers might have been "To exchange ideas," "To create synergy," "To accelerate the launching process"), members would have been aware of the obstacles in their communication right from the start (such as language and one-way presentations).

Another valuable insight is an awareness about the time required for learning to be assimilated in order to change behavior. The "magic" of learning and changing group behavior takes more than one day. The cycle needs to be repeated several times.

FACILITATING GLOBAL TEAMS AT GENERAL MOTORS

In 1994 General Motors created Global Task Teams (GTT) as a way to build groups of eight to ten high-potential employees who could work together to address important organizational issues. Over the past four years, tasks and sites have included the following:

SITE	TASK
India	To contribute to the design and implementation of a lean manufacturing system and related support systems
Indonesia	To develop manufacturing systems for new operations
North America	To identify marketing indicators for new products
Australia	To design a material flow process for a new body shop
England	To review marketing strategy for improving customer satisfaction

After the initial launch, each team spends four weeks visiting the companies that represent the "best practices" of the task it has been assigned. The next eight weeks are then spent at the GM site developing what the team has learned as a result of its benchmarking efforts. At the end of the three-month program, the team makes recommendations and, in some cases, begins the implementation process. Also, time for extensive reflection is undertaken to optimize the learning from the experience and anticipate their reentry into positions at GM.

There are several critical junctions during the three-month program in which the two GM facilitators meet with the Global Task Teams. On these occasions, the two facilitators help the team explore how effectively they are working as a group, what they hope to achieve, what they have learned, and how they might apply this learning to their home unit (Dixon, 1998). Throughout the program, but especially during closure week, team members, with the assistance of the facilitators, provide each other with in-depth feedback on a wide variety of leadership behavior. The facilitators also interview key people at the site to gain insight about the team and provide this information to the team. The Global Task Teams have earned a growing reputation within General Motors for the quality of their work and the quality of the teams.

POWER AND VALUE OF A TEAM FACILITATOR

Facilitators assist global teams and intervene in a variety of ways that can significantly improve the team's performance as well as the working environment. Changing a member's experience from negative—and thus too discouraging to want to be involved in future teams—to positive and pro-

GLOBAL TEAM FACILITATORS

ductive will assuredly cause more and more people to want to be part of global teams.

A growing number of other companies (Boeing, Unilever, Whirlpool, Qantas Airlines) are now using facilitators to optimize the power of their global teams. And as we have seen, facilitators play a key role in helping the team to improve its assessment and feedback capabilities—a topic explored in Chapter 10.

Chapter 10

Measurement and Feedback Systems

Measurement and feedback systems are vitally important tools for global teams that seek to be productive. They allow the team to view its progress and operations and thereby establish accountability. Measurement and feedback can likewise serve as part of total quality management systems since they track how well the team is accomplishing its goals and implementing its strategies. Aside from improving team performance, measurement and feedback systems are also used as the basis for appraising individual performance.

In this chapter we explore three elements of measurement and feedback for global teams: the development of measurement and feedback systems; how culture affects these systems; and guidelines for designing and implementing these systems. To illustrate the key concepts of global measurement and feedback systems, we will look at case studies from BP, Colgate-Palmolive, and Glaxo-Wellcome.

DESIGNING EFFECTIVE MEASUREMENT AND FEEDBACK SYSTEMS

To design an effective measurement and feedback system, four elements must be incorporated. *First:* Establish linkage to the organization's business strategy. This requires senior management to communicate such a strategy clearly to the team—which, in turn, must understand why the strategy is necessary. The global team can then determine how its objectives can be aligned with the strategy.

Second: Incorporate customer needs. If a team is designing a new product or service, customer needs should become part of the measurement system. Obtaining direct information from customers adds to the relevance of team metrics.

Third: Ensure team participation in the development of measures. Team members must adopt the measures as their own if they are to improve their performance. By assigning a measure to an individual team member, you can avoid the "it's theirs" attitude toward the measure. Each team member becomes, in effect, the subject of the measure and leads the team in efforts to improve performance on that measure.

Fourth: Use feedback for improving team productivity. Like any tool, feedback can be used positively or negatively. If it is used for motivating team members to meet the challenge of overcoming gaps in performance, the result is positive. If feedback focuses exclusively on negative performance and ignores progress, team members will become indifferent or even resistant (Jones and Moffett, 1999).

In addressing these four basic elements, it's useful to remember that team performance can be evaluated in two dimensions: how well the team works together (team process) and how successful the team is in meeting its stated objectives (team outcomes) (Davison and Ward, 1999). *Team process* can be measured by such factors as how well the team creates and sustains motivation, utilizes the knowledge and skills of team members, or manages its relationship with clients. *Team outcomes* can be measured by the number of units produced at an acceptable level of quality, the number of innovations and their diffusion, and milestones reached within scheduled deadlines and budgets.

Some measures do not distinguish between process and outcome. Instead they focus on certain behavioral outcomes. For measuring a team leader's effectiveness, for example, this would mean developing measures of effective problem solving or maintaining strategic focus (Davison and Ward, 1999)—or, alternatively, assessing certain attributes such as whether team members correct each other's mistakes (Brannick and Prince, 1997).

MEASUREMENT AND FEEDBACK SYSTEMS

MEASURING BP'S GLOBAL TEAM PERFORMANCE

BP's European Gas Business Development team (EGBD), formed in 1991, was charged with developing a business plan for locating, producing, transporting, and selling natural gas on the European continent. Developing a performance measurement system, however, proved to be very difficult (Snow et al., 1996). It would be 1997 at the earliest that any gas would reach the European market. Therefore, evaluating the team on such hard measures as revenues generated or market share increase would make little sense. As a result, the team's performance at the start could only be assessed subjectively. Areas of measurement initially focused on progress in negotiations, the ability to add staff during an overall company downsizing, and the continued support of BP's board of directors.

While teams are often evaluated in terms of their outputs—as if the only measure of a basketball team's performance is whether it wins a game—this overlooks the fact that outcomes are influenced not only by teamwork but also by factors outside the team (Brannick and Prince, 1997). If all such factors are present, team *process* may give a truer picture than outcome measures, although both types are needed for comprehensive evaluation schemes.

Measurement systems should be built upon a solid understanding of assessment theory, the dynamic nature of teamwork, principles of observation and data collection, and standards of reliability and validity. Table 7 on the next page shows how each of these issues can be applied to a measurement system for global teams.

Measurement and feedback are essential because organizations know little about the processes within teams that would account for the very real differences in their performance. Developing measures that reveal the process factors associated with good performance can thus improve team performance.

Theories of teamwork can be used to develop global team process measures, but incorporating actual team experiences is equally important (Baker and Salas, 1997). Since teams evolve their own practices, measurement must take into account the timing of the evaluation. A snapshot reading is not likely to provide as much guidance as a series of measurements over time.

TABLE 7
Principles and Applications for Measuring Team Skills

ISSUE	PRINCIPLES AND APPLICATIONS
Theory	Full understanding of team performance requires behavioral, cognitive, and attitudinal measures
	Development of team performance measures must be guided in part by theory and in part by empirical research
Group maturation/ development	Measures must capture the dynamic nature of teamwork
	Measures and measurement tools must reflect the team's maturation process
	Measures must account for team members' experience with a team
Observation	Team performance is not simply what team members do
	Observation is critical for measuring team behavioral skills and providing feedback
Application	Performance measures must be developed, implemented, and evaluated for a wide variety of teams in a wide range of settings
	Psychometric data must be collected on all new measures of team performance
Rigor	Judges and measures must be reliable
Performance	Team performance measures must predict team outcomes
	Team performance measures must look as if they assess team performance

Source: Adapted from Baker and Salas (1997).

MEASUREMENT AND FEEDBACK FOR COLGATE'S GLOBAL HR TEAM

Colgate-Palmolive is a $9 billion global company with over 38,000 employees serving people in more than 200 countries. As Colgate-Palmolive globalizes as a company, there is a greater and greater need to begin standardization of best practices on a global scale. A core group, Total Productivity Maintenance (TPM), was established in 1996 to keep up to date about the best technology worldwide and how the company could use it.

A four-member global team was formed to ensure the relevance and quality of a new global training program on TPM as well as help Colgate attain its long-term goals in productivity improvement. One of the team's first activities was to design a training program for transferring best practices on a global scale.

The team began by training a group of people who in turn trained others. This process led to a rapid cascade of training throughout the organization. The team worked closely with the Global Education and Training Unit to be sure that team training was standardized.

We undertook a number of quality assurance procedures to be sure the training was effective. Our team also assisted in training the TPM unit to upgrade its use of technology. Although the TPM program is built on the Japanese system of total quality management, the global team made appropriate adaptations so that the methods and implementation would be global while the training materials and delivery would be adapted for each culture.

By late 1999, the TPM global team had measured and received positive feedback on the following activities:

- Performance indicators that were used to measure the success of the training
- Certification standards for those training in TPM
- Development of a 5-$1/2$-day training program during which the participants demonstrate their technical competence and ability to deliver the training program on their own
- Fourteen workshops delivered to trainers who in turn delivered an additional forty training programs to Colgate-Palmolive people worldwide
- Assurance of quality and consistency of content, standards, and procedures

TAILORING MEASUREMENT AND FEEDBACK FOR GLOBAL TEAMS

Organizations have been turning increasingly to global teams to perform a variety of critical tasks or services. This use of global teams has often been unjustified, however, since organizations have never developed valid measurement and feedback systems to evaluate how their teams are performing. Most evaluation systems still tend to focus on individual or organizational, not team, performances. Yet global teams have special characteristics that should be accounted for in setting up evaluation criteria. There are three key decisions to be made in designing measurement and feedback systems for global teams: what to measure, when to measure, and how to measure (Baker and Salas, 1997).

The first task is to distinguish between team performance and outcomes. Performance means what goes on as the team does its work. This requires looking at such factors as levels of motivation, use of team members' knowledge and skills, and how the team relates to its sponsoring organization. Effectiveness measures are commonly understood to assess both the quantity and the quality of outputs—providing information on how the team solves problems and how it adheres to deadlines and budgets (Davison and Ward, 1999).

The how and when of measurement should be determined in relation to the team's mission and its composition. In harmony with the whole concept of self-management, the team itself should be involved in developing the criteria for measuring the degree to which it is successful (Davison and Ward, 1999). By assessing its strengths and weaknesses, the team can use this information as a benchmark for devising criteria that will measure improvement from a baseline. When measuring, it is very important for global teams to focus on different views of professional cultures and leadership styles.

If measurement and feedback focus only on outcomes and are used too early in the team's life cycle, the evaluation may be discouraging and even damaging to team morale. If this leads to the team's termination, all the organization's work in developing knowledge on team effectiveness could be lost for use by future teams (Davison and Ward, 1999).

To avoid such pitfalls, successful companies develop measurement systems at the team level. This assures that team members understand the measures and can use them for self-improvement. At its initial meetings, the global team should focus on developing the key criteria by which its performance will be assessed. Agreement on what and how to

MEASUREMENT AND FEEDBACK SYSTEMS

measure takes longer with global teams since they have representatives from diverse cultures who have differing perspectives about what constitutes success and appropriate behavior.

While most performance evaluation systems provide feedback and even link incentives to improvements, the simple use of feedback for rewards does not necessarily influence members' motivation or the team's problem-solving effectiveness. If teams interpret negative feedback as failure, this can lead members to blame forces outside the team, other team members, or even the measure itself. But if the data are presented as a tool the team can use to analyze precisely where its performance or strategy can be improved, then team productivity is likely to improve (Jones and Moffett, 1999).

As the team moves on its life cycle, its leaders and facilitators need to ensure that the feedback mechanisms adopted as part of the evaluation system are utilized. If the degree of participation by certain members is to be measured, for example, videotapes of sessions (or the facilitator's observations) can be used to convey the reality (Davison and Ward, 1999). Here are some guidelines for developing a measurement and feedback system for a global team (adapted from McDermott et al., 1998):

- Ensure that the measures you select are aligned with the organization's mission and vision.
- Include team goals and objectives.
- Reflect key stakeholders' expectations.
- Include current benchmark data and the team's reaction, learning, behavior, and results.
- Finalize the measures with your stakeholders.
- Establish the current level (baseline) for each metric. If baselines don't exist, do a survey of "perceptions."
- Establish an improvement goal (benchmark) for each metric. These should be set at realistic levels and pegged to a future date, such as one year.

MEASURING RESULTS WITH GLAXO-WELLCOME GLOBAL TEAMS

Karen Ward

There are a variety of reasons why the Glaxo-Wellcome team has been able to work so successfully to date. Above all, this team has been willing to abide by one of the golden rules of complex teams: Start slow to end fast—or start fast and never end at all. In practice this means paying attention to task and process simultaneously throughout the life cycle of the team.

In today's short-term environment, organizations often put pressure on teams to deliver. But deliver what? At best, solutions that don't have buy-in from key stakeholders across the organization or solutions that have ignored innovative opportunities; at worst, solutions that destroy long-term value. Yet experience has illustrated that where teams take the time to really understand and value their diversity instead of trying to minimize it, they ultimately deliver higher-quality solutions within budget and on schedule. This team has interspersed its face-to-face meetings with activities to help team members understand each other better, manage change effectively, work apart optimally, and develop creative and novel solutions.

These just-in-time development activities are team-building activities, as well, and help members to value the diverse views in the team. They are learning to value the uniqueness of each individual on the team and regard their diversity as strength. The team acknowledges that it is a microcosm of the wider organization—and if the team cannot see the sense of a particular line of thinking, then it is unlikely to gain acceptance in the organization.

In order to engage everyone and, at the same time, meet the needs of the new company, the team identified its key goal: individual site improvement based on various measures of performance. Although the team as a whole agreed on the most logical measures as guidelines, each member would meet with his or her site team to determine the most useful measure at that site in terms of improving performance.

Three significant measures of performance for the entire project were determined:

1. Quality of finished product—either through quality control efforts (stability, counts, damaged product) or through wasted batches.

MEASUREMENT AND FEEDBACK SYSTEMS

2. Volume—although the team was careful not to compare one site to another. Sites were measured against themselves with a continuous improvement mind-set. The name of the game was to be continuously raising the bar for each site. Obviously team members and production managers felt compelled to look good compared to other sites. But in reality, environmental factors beyond their control would sometimes prevent exact comparisons.

3. The time necessary to get a plant qualified for production of a new product. Each site could determine when it would be ready. Scheduling of inspections, however, depended on the regulatory agency.

Best Practices

Based on the experience of numerous global teams, a number of effective practices have been identified for measuring and providing feedback. Let's summarize the best practices for developing a team measurement and feedback system:

- Use the measurement system to capture the business strategy.
- Bring in the customer's perspective.
- Use team participation.
- Use constructive management review.
- Align individual goals with team goals.
- Use the roles of team leader and coach to facilitate feedback meetings.
- Frame team performance feedback as a source of motivation and as data for solving problems.
- Promote the use of performance feedback in improving team performance rather than evaluating individual performance.
- Consider providing incentives for team performance.

CULTURE AND FEEDBACK

In considering the timing and method of obtaining feedback, remember the influence of low-context and high-context styles of communication and their impact on measurement systems. Germans, as an example of a low-context communication culture, may value a clear, detailed written report. Someone from a high-context culture such as that in Brazil, however, may prefer to talk about the subject informally and get a graphic overview of highlights.

Another important factor to remember in using feedback with global teams is that reactions may very well depend on the cultural style of communicating criticism. Some cultures prefer direct confrontation and discussion of problems because it occurs in the context of a personal relationship. In others, written communication carries more weight (Devereaux and Johansen, 1994).

To evaluate the competency attained by a team member versus what is required for the position, it's necessary to develop a culturally reliable database of norms for that position and culture. For example, let's consider measuring the warmth, approachability, and friendliness of a salesperson. If we were to measure an Italian salesperson against English norms, that person would be rated as uncontrollably emotional. A German salesperson measured against French norms might be judged humorless and cold. But Wilson Learning, a global consulting firm, has developed fifteen different databases that enable them to measure German behavior against German norms, French behavior against French norms, and so on. Wilson Learning tests about 500 people in each culture to develop such a database.

Another aspect of evaluation developed by Wilson Learning is the value of a culture's rating compared to other cultures. There is a great reluctance among the Japanese to rate anyone at the top end of the scale, for example, since the Japanese simply do not deal in superlatives the way Americans do. To compensate, Wilson decided that a Japanese rating of "4" equaled "7" in the United States. Likewise a "10" in Indonesia might equal a "7" in the United States (Sheehan and Murray, 1990).

MEASUREMENT AND FEEDBACK SYSTEMS

GUIDELINES FOR MEASUREMENT AND FEEDBACK SYSTEMS

Measurement and feedback must function together in a well-designed evaluation system. To ensure that all aspects of the system (the what, how, and when) are considered during the design and implementation of a continuous improvement program, the organization and global team should follow these ten principles:

1. The measurement system must incorporate the organization's business strategy and be clear to team members.

2. Measures should relate to the tasks, time, location, team composition, level of experience, and other distinguishing factors of a global team.

3. Measures must be adjusted to fit culturally different views of what constitutes success and high performance.

4. Global teams should take part in the design of their measurement system as this will develop a greater acceptance among members.

5. Make individuals on the team responsible for improvement in specific performance and outcome measures. Another way of creating buy-in is to have a steering committee from key groups in the sponsoring organization guide the team in developing measures. Dialogue with management also creates buy-in on that side and encourages adoption of measures that will have credibility in the organization.

6. Management needs to keep reviewing measurement systems to ensure they are capturing elements essential to their goals.

7. Align individual goals with team goals at the outset by having the team agree on a common purpose.

8. Present feedback as information for solving problems rather than for evaluating individual performance. Avoid focusing exclusively on negative performance.

9. Use team evaluations to determine how well the team strategy is working rather than how well individuals are performing.

10. Allow sufficient time in the early stages of the team's life cycle for principles 3 and 4 to be accomplished before using the system to judge whether the team is progressing toward its targeted outcomes.

FUTURE TRENDS

Due to global competition and the growing expectations of customers, a number of future trends are affecting the whole subject of measurement and feedback. Jones and Moffett (1999) suggest how measurement and feedback systems are likely to be implemented in the future:

- *Automation:* Currently most measurement systems for teams require some manual data input and may lag behind real-time events by a week or more. Greater automation will replace much manual input and approach real-time feedback for most team measures.

- *Strategy:* Team measurement systems will become more clearly tied to business strategy so that each team can see how well its strategy is working (and how well it supports the company strategy).

- *Team cooperation:* The measurement systems of different teams in a business unit will become more integrated so that team cooperation is reflected in the measurement systems.

- *Customers:* The boundary between customers and teams will continue to dissolve with regard to measurement and feedback.

- *Business savvy:* Effective measurement systems will engage teams in greater understanding of the business.

- *Business partners:* High-performance teams will act more like business partners than employees by monitoring and improving their performance measures.

FEEDBACK AND REWARDS

In 1985 Michael LeBoeuf wrote a best-selling book titled *The Greatest Management Principle in the World*. The book's main character discovers the most powerful axiom of all organization life—"That which gets rewarded gets done"—as well as a corollary principle stating "That which gets measured gets rewarded." If we want people to join global teams, we have to recognize the importance of these two business truisms. We must therefore not only measure global team success. We also have to reward it—otherwise it won't happen. In this chapter we've examined the measurement and feedback systems for global teams. How to *reward* the efforts of global team members is the subject of Chapter 11.

Chapter 11

Team-Oriented Assessment and Rewards

Although what one sees as a reward or "deems rewarding" may differ from culture to culture, the fact remains that as human beings we all respond to those people, events, and systems that reward us. This is just as true for teams, whether global or local, as it is for individuals.

As a result of this truism, organizations and global team leaders must recognize the importance of creating a reward system that will motivate each and every member of the global team. To assure that the reward system benefits the team members as well as the organization, corporate and team leaders should develop a system that aligns with the company's global business strategies, encourages team collaboration as well as individual initiatives, and is universally fair yet culturally sensitive.

In this chapter we'll look at the basic principles of team-based assessment and reward systems. The chapter then examines how culture and other elements inherent in global teams affect these systems. As well, the assessment and reward systems of Philips, P&G, and Andersen Consulting are presented to illustrate best practices on this topic.

ASSESSMENTS AND COMPENSATION

Today's successful organizations evaluate employees on their performance in teams as well as individually. As a result of this new and growing trend, HR leaders must rethink how to reward and compensate people—especially on their contributions to their team's performance.

This new form of compensation is frequently called "team-based rewards" or "team-based pay." Rewarding team performance does not, of course, mean abandoning individual rewards. In fact, team compensation schemes should recognize individual differences in the contribution of each member of the team. In general, team reward schemes have two main goals: to encourage effective participation on teams and to develop the skills and competencies needed to solve problems in the team mode. Compensation for good results can have a positive impact on both the individual and the team. As Table 8 shows, six different factors (attraction, motivation, skill development, culture, structure, and cost) can affect the impact of pay on the performance of individuals and teams.

In designing a team compensation system—particularly one for a global team—consideration should be given to several critical factors:

Time required: Developing a complete system of evaluation and compensation can take several years. Caudron (1994) recommends no more than a year's time lag between starting a team and beginning a reward system.

Types of teams: There are different types of teams—such as product development teams, temporary problem-solving teams, or teams that carry out work processes. Each may require different incentives (Gross, 1995; Lee, 1997).

Evaluation criteria: Accurate and objective criteria for appraising, recording, and reporting team performance are a prerequisite to designing an effective team compensation scheme (Bartol and Hagmann, 1992).

Monetary vs. nonmonetary rewards: Recognition that motivates team members can be in the form of either pay or nonmonetary rewards. In fact, noncash rewards are recommended as the primary type of recognition for all types of teams (Gross, 1995).

Differing perceptions and motivations: Team members are accustomed to different motivations based on experiences in their home culture and work environment.

TABLE 8
Impact of Pay on Performance

FACTOR	INDIVIDUAL MERIT	TEAM INCENTIVE
Attraction	Good for high performers	Good if team does well
Motivation	Good line of sight (behavior leads to attractive outcomes)	Moderate line of sight (behavior leads to attractive outcomes)
Skill development	Encourages learning skills that lead to rewarded performance	Encourages team skills
Culture	Performance-oriented, job-focused	Team-focused
Structure	Individual accountability	Team integration
Cost	High if significant merit awards are given	High if significant rewards are given

Source: Adapted from Lawler (1999).

ANDERSEN'S GUIDELINES FOR ASSESSING GLOBAL TEAMS

Andersen Consulting works with hundreds of companies all over the world in a variety of human resource areas, including performance assessment and compensation systems. The firm offers the following guidelines to organizations in assessing and rewarding members of global teams:

- Standardize performance measurement systems across all locations, make adjustments with guidelines to account for local nuances, and base compensation on performance and achievement of goals.
- Consider nonmonetary forms of compensation for cultural reasons (flextime, vacation periods, and so forth).
- Be aware of the differences between expatriates and locals. Coach expatriates on how to address these issues with colleagues.
- Reward expatriate knowledge and skills when promoting global career opportunities in newsletters, new releases, project updates, and the like.

PERFORMANCE APPRAISAL SYSTEMS

Very few organizations have effective measures for evaluating the teams they establish. Where they do exist, they often focus on only part of the picture—the output of the team in terms of the targets established. This can lead to overlooking other positive results of team performance, such as learning conveyed to the organization. For this reason, appraisal systems should recognize two different categories of results: team performance and outcome effectiveness.

A product development team may, for example, come up with a product that for reasons beyond the team's control is not successfully manufactured or marketed. Relying purely on outcome effectiveness would force us to rate this team's effectiveness at zero. But what if this team has discovered ways to develop products more quickly or to make global teams function better? This learning can be passed on to other teams and will help the company succeed in the long run. Davison and Ward (1999) have cited several performance measures that could be set by global teams:

- The team has set clear goals, targets, and time lines and adhered to them.
- The team has managed conflict constructively.
- The team has effectively handled unexpected crises and deviations from the initial plan.
- The team has informed and invited feedback.
- The team has clarified the external factors that affect its performance and has created mechanisms for staying abreast of changes in these factors.

After recognizing the elements of team performance and outcome effectiveness, the designer of a compensation system should consider carefully a process that, at a minimum, involves:

- Obtaining a commitment from management for evaluating team performance as well as outcome measures
- Securing the participation of the team's sponsors as well as its leaders and members

- Identifying specific objectives the team is expected to perform on the way to its goal

Incorporating these elements in the process will improve your chances of arriving at effective appraisal tools. The major benefits of paying attention to the process are that it will reveal valuable information to the organization. The sponsor and team will learn, for example, what the team can and cannot control. This is useful in determining what team members can fairly be held accountable for. The process will also reveal how team members from different countries view the desirability of certain outcomes. Even the uncovering of potential conflict between cost-imposed goals versus quality can be beneficial. It may alert team members that they may have to push and persuade for consideration of one goal over the other. Finally, in the early stages the collaborative process will reveal critical barriers to the success of a global team effort (Davison and Ward, 1999).

THE IMPACT OF CULTURE

Apart from these general principles of design, there are special factors to consider when appraising the performance of global teams. Given the broad theater of operations of global companies, the participation of team members, leaders, and sponsors in the design process may involve use of questionnaires and surveys. Yet different nationalities may be more or less forthcoming depending on the method used to obtain their input. Some cultures feel it is improper to criticize authority figures or make suggestions. Some are more willing to do so on paper; others prefer addressing the person directly.

Such cultural differences raise a warning flag about trying to design a one-size-fits-all compensation scheme that can be used across the whole organization. The better course is to support teams in establishing their own performance measures or evaluation criteria.

Clearly a global organization, to be successful in designing team compensation systems, must give weight to these cultural factors. To do so requires time. Managers should recognize that team members from diverse cultures have significantly more viewpoints to resolve before they begin work. For this reason, the motto "start slow to end fast" applies—especially to evaluating the performance of global teams.

GLOBAL TEAMS REWARDED AT PROCTER & GAMBLE

P&G, the world's largest manufacturer of household products, has recently reorganized around global business units instead of geographic regions. About half of its sales come from outside the United States. Recently the company created a cluster of global work teams called Corporate New Venture (CNV), an autonomous idea lab. Its mission is to encourage new ideas for products and put them into speedy production by funding the best ideas. Ideas bubbling up from P&G's workforce of 110,000 are routed to a CNV innovation team via My Idea, a corporate collaboration network. CNV teams then put the ideas under the microscope—using the Internet to analyze markets, demographics, and cost information to make sure a new product idea is feasible.

Once the team decides to go ahead, a project is launched within days. The CNV people have the authority to tap any resources in the company to bring a product to market—including the brainpower of the company's engineers, scattered at twenty-three sites around the world.

The program already has delivered results. So far, CNV has put fifty-eight products into the marketplace. One of CNV's first items, a new cleaning product called "Swiffer," got pushed out the door in just ten months—less than half the usual time for new products. Swiffer, a disposable cleaning cloth that generates electrostatic charges to attract dust and dirt, was dreamed up during a novel collaboration between P&G's paper and cleaning-agent experts. The team members were pulled together to start talking in person and via the Internet. They were challenged to think more broadly beyond their typical topics: detergents and diapers. It was an exercise in speed—in breaking down the company's traditional division-by-division territories to come up with new ideas. Compensation has been a key factor in making these projects work. At P&G, employees who submit winning ideas are rewarded with stock options.

UNIQUE CHALLENGES

Those involved in designing global team compensation systems should consider a variety of factors when arriving at a scheme that can be applied globally. Among these are:

- *Varying pay schemes and scales:* Offering more money for participation on a global team may create a problem when a member from a low-income country goes home and faces a pay cut. Higher compensation of senior team members or those from high-income countries may demoralize the rest of the global team.

- *Differing tax and legal requirements:* The laws of the home country may produce different results for employees receiving bonuses—for example, monetary versus nonmonetary rewards such as perks.

- *Different cultural views of fairness:* Americans, for example, generally feel it unfair if a large part of their pay depends on the performance of others; with Japanese, this is less of a problem.

- *Part-time employees:* For team members who work part-time on several teams, the compensation they receive for performance may be relatively minor and thus less of an incentive (Davison and Ward, 1999).

GUIDELINES

There is no easy formula for handling these challenges. A review of successful compensation schemes for global teams, however, does yield a number of principles that can help you avoid the common pitfalls:

- Recognize local differences in HR policies. This can be done by making the compensation and appraisal of individual team members relevant to their home-based workplaces. Evaluations should be done by home country managers, therefore, with input from team leaders and members. Because this may lead to varying rates of pay within the team and be difficult to administer, applying this principle may require trade-offs.

- Combine individual, team, and home country rewards. This also involves balancing global and local concerns.

- Reward organizational learning. Appraisal and reward systems often are keyed to definitive results that support the firm's strategic objectives. Systems should also support learning that leads to long-term innovation rather than just achievement of short-term targets.

- Avoid one-size-fits-all solutions. Make systems flexible to reflect the type of team and the degree to which team success depends on interaction among members.

- Involve team members in the process of devising the appraisal and compensation system.

- Obtain management's commitment to the evaluation and compensation scheme.

- Consider both team and individual rewards, taking into account variations in local pay scales and reward systems.

- Find out how members from different cultures view various team objectives, performance measures, and types of compensation.

- Make the system specific, equitable, and timely—then communicate it clearly.

- Stress nonmonetary rewards as well as bonuses and other forms of cash compensation.

- Take the time necessary to implement these guidelines—even if it takes a year after a team is organized to put the compensation system in place.

Oddou and Mendenhall (1988) suggest additional steps in appraising and rewarding an employee's performance:

- Determine the difficulty of the assignment. For example, it's generally much harder for an American to work in China than in Canada. The degree of difficulty depends on such variables as language, cultural differences, and economic and political stability. Remember that local situations, events, and differences may make success much tougher to achieve and require greater effort with fewer results.

- Objectify the performance assessment by using former expatriates from the same location and involving on-site and home-site managers. Recognize that appraisal by a supervisor of another culture will involve that culture's values, ways of acting, and judgments. Take into account input from co-workers within the culture in which they are working. (These evaluations can be problematic, however, since they'll be assessing the person's performance from their own cultural frame of reference and set of expectations. Participative management, for example, might be seen as incompetent because there's not enough control and not enough expertise.)

- Consider all the aspects of members' experiences—and remember that they are not only performing a specific function but are also broadening their understanding of the firm's total operations.

- In determining pay, local markets generally are the biggest determinant of equity. A team member in Lagos doing the same job as a member in Houston may be paid one-tenth the salary. In determining fair compensation, the organization needs to consider the cost of living, the replacement cost of hiring and firing, and the availability of qualified labor. Within local markets, companies should maintain equitable pay according to job class and tenure with the company.

GLOBAL AND TEAM-ORIENTED REWARD SYSTEMS AT PHILIPS

Philips, a Dutch-based electronics company, recognizes that global teams are crucial for its survival in the semiconductor industry—and thus has put new emphasis on its employees' being able to work in cross-functional and cross-cultural teams. What's more, job rotation has always been the heart of Philips' philosophy of management development. It is seen as increasingly important in the firm's efforts to develop interdisciplinary skills and global perspectives. The candidates considered to have the most potential for tomorrow's top management positions can be expected to be sent abroad for at least three years.

A recent variation on job rotation is the assignment of Philips managers to ventures with other companies. Those posted to these global team assignments have the opportunity to experience company cultures and practices different from their own. Transferring people in and out of these ventures contributes both to the person's professional growth and to the expansion of the company's perspective as a whole. On-the-job training coupled with experience on global teams is the core of career development at Philips.

Philips uses the following components to reward managers who work in global cross-cultural teams and settings:

- The performance appraisal system has become increasingly objective in an effort to assign demonstrable, job-related, culturally sensitive criteria to the evaluations. The emphasis on objective performance evaluation is spreading to include corporate staff functions that previously were considered too difficult to evaluate in objective terms.

- The potential appraisal system is more subjective since the outcomes are a combination of judgment and hypotheses about the future. Nevertheless, it is the critical part of career planning and development for both the individual and the company.

- The judgment of managers in selecting potential candidates for today's global teams and tomorrow's top management positions is crucial—and it's a responsibility that is taken very seriously. Responsibility for the management development program is therefore spread throughout the entire organization. Line managers shoulder the largest share, since they must perform the evaluations and appraisals (Van Houten, 1990).

A QUESTION OF BALANCE

Working in a global environment requires very different organizational policies, practices, and systems in order to support teams with members drawn from different cultures and work environments. Since compensation is a strong motivator for changing behavior, organizations need to align their reward programs specifically to encourage both high-quality team performance and individual performance. The challenge is to balance global team reward incentives with local practices.

Chapter 12

Building Global Teams for the Twenty-first Century

Thus far in this book we have focused primarily on global teams from the internal perspective. In presenting the GlobalTeams Model, we have examined the nine key components of successful global teams. But for a global team to be properly created, developed, and maintained, the sponsoring organization must provide long-term, corporate-wide commitment and support. All too often, management underestimates the impact of global teams on the organization. And rarely is management aware of the level of support they require. In this chapter we look at global teams from the perspective of what an organization can do to foster and sustain them.

In a recent survey of global teams, 85 percent of the surveyed companies agreed that for global teams to succeed, top management must be directly involved in the effort or at least support it. Despite this awareness of the importance of corporate support, very few companies—primarily in manufacturing sectors and firms located outside the United States—were building and supporting their global teams (McShulskis, 1996). Is it any wonder, then, that most global teams are not achieving their potential?

Overcoming the five major challenges faced by global teams—cultural diversity, geographic distance, coordination and control, communications, and teamness—is extremely difficult. Too many organizations fail and never get to appreciate the value and power of successful

GLOBAL TEAMS

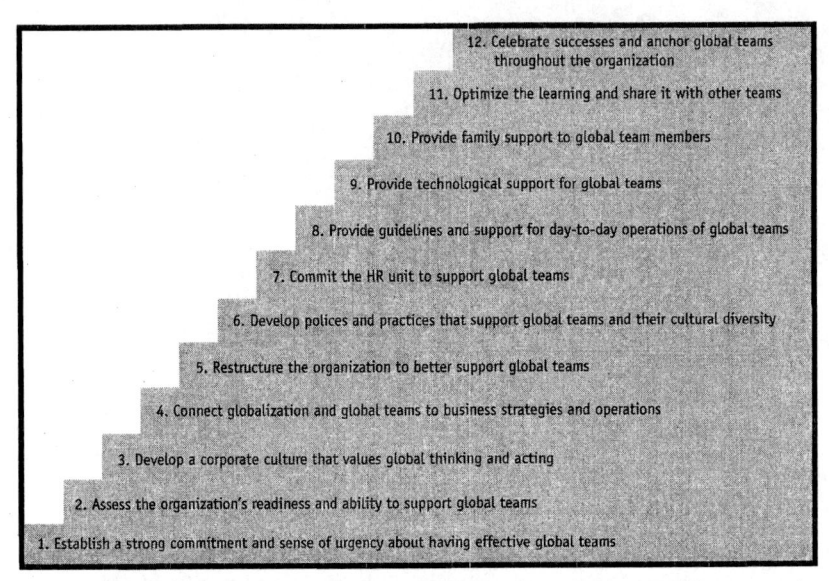

12. Celebrate successes and anchor global teams throughout the organization
11. Optimize the learning and share it with other teams
10. Provide family support to global team members
9. Provide technological support for global teams
8. Provide guidelines and support for day-to-day operations of global teams
7. Commit the HR unit to support global teams
6. Develop polices and practices that support global teams and their cultural diversity
5. Restructure the organization to better support global teams
4. Connect globalization and global teams to business strategies and operations
3. Develop a corporate culture that values global thinking and acting
2. Assess the organization's readiness and ability to support global teams
1. Establish a strong commitment and sense of urgency about having effective global teams

Figure 6 • STEPS AND STRATEGIES FOR BUILDING GLOBAL TEAMS

global teams. The organization must therefore have a systematic and comprehensive strategy for building global teams and providing the necessary support to sustain them. In this chapter we examine twelve steps that organizations can undertake to build and support global teams. (See Figure 5.)

STEP 1: ESTABLISH A STRONG COMMITMENT AND SENSE OF URGENCY

As demonstrated in Chapter 1, global teams are critical for a company's survival and success. Leadership, however, needs to establish this importance and sense of urgency throughout the organization. Research has shown that most successful change efforts begin when people within the organization look seriously at the company's competitive situation, market position, technological trends, or financial performance and realize that a great crisis—or opportunity—looms. This first step is essential since getting a transformation program started requires a strong realization of urgency on the part of many individuals. Unlike as in other organizational transformation efforts, top leadership must jump to the forefront and let people know that diverse and highly competent global teams are essential to their corporate success.

Most companies never get their transformation off the ground because they fail at this first phase. What are some of the reasons for these failures?

- Executives underestimate how hard it can be to drive people out of their comfort zones—especially zones built within cultural cocoons.
- Leaders lack patience to handle inertia or resistance to the use of global teams.
- Top leadership becomes paralyzed by the downside possibilities of the impending changes: senior employees will become defensive, key people will refuse to take part, morale will drop, events will spin out of control, short-term business results will be jeopardized, and so on.
- Managers are afraid to take the risks involved in creating the new corporate culture, strategies, and structures associated with global teams.

This commitment must not only be based on the urgency of creating and using global teams. It should be based, as well, on the many benefits that will accrue to the organization, to employees, and to shareholders. Leadership needs to believe that global companies with global teams will be exciting and fulfilling places in which to work and learn. Top leadership at Pfizer, for example, urges a "strong commitment by all key stakeholder groups to support their global teams and to develop mutual expectations and measures of success." Senior executives "must provide visible support and commitment" to Pfizer's global teams. And Colgate-Palmolive, as shown in the following case study, has also made a strong commitment to global teams.

COLGATE-PALMOLIVE'S COMMITMENT TO GLOBAL TEAMS

Reuben Mark, Colgate-Palmolive's chairman and chief executive officer, has made global teams a sine qua non for the company's success. In the 1998 annual report he writes:

Experienced Colgate people across all disciplines and regions are working in a collective commitment to drive our profitable growth. Global teamwork is at the heart of reaping the benefits of our global activities. Colgate salespeople are also sharing best practices with their peers as we move to team-based selling for large multi-country trade customers. Collaboration is equally important for new tightly focused groups of research scientists and marketing experts working together from various locations to develop tomorrow's products. Colgate people in the U.S., sharing knowledge and learning to work in teams, are the first to have been trained in "Valuing Colgate People," an award-winning program recognized by the U.S. Department of Labor.

Members of Colgate's Total Productivity Maintenance global team, when interviewed for this book, echoed the importance of having top-level support. They emphasize the following points:

- Get everyone on board at the beginning—from the top to the bottom of the company.
- Commitment may not always be there. You may need to fight for it sometimes, but it is critical.
- Be sure to ask for support and recognition from top levels of the company. In our case, we needed them to understand the value of technology for the improvement and success of Colgate's business.
- Global projects may take a great deal of time as you obtain worldwide input, develop solid strategies, and implement efficiently. Don't rush something that's important if you want global success. Because American culture demands results yesterday, many global teams tend to take the low-hanging, easy-to-reach fruit. If it takes ten years to get to world-class quality, take the time. That's why up-front, strong organizational support is so necessary.

STEP 2: ASSESS THE ORGANIZATION'S READINESS

As in most organizational transformation efforts, a critical early step is to assess the organization's readiness and ability to build and use global teams. It's essential to identify internal strengths and weaknesses as well as external threats and opportunities. Although many organizations may informally or haphazardly assess some aspect of their globalization efforts, the top companies recognize the importance of undertaking a comprehensive, systematic examination of their global capability and readiness. The organization must also decide if it will begin with a few pilot global teams—or go immediately into employing global teams for all operations.

The GlobalTeams Capability and Readiness Profile (Appendix A) has been used by a number of organizations seeking to develop and deploy global teams. The instrument examines each of the nine Global-Teams components discussed in this book.

STEP 3: DEVELOP A CORPORATE CULTURE

David Whitwam, CEO of Whirlpool, declared that the key to globalizing the organization was to get everyone to think and act globally, not just a few. Developing a global mind-set—allowing people to exchange ideas and implement activities easily across cultural and personal borders, to accept other cultural perspectives, and to join or support global teams—is essential.

Leaders in the organization should be encouraged to continually expand their knowledge, develop a high conceptual capacity to deal with the complexity of global organizations, be extremely flexible, strive to be sensitive to cultural diversity, intuit decisions with less-than-perfect information, and have a strong capacity for reflection. The emphasis should be on balancing global and local needs and being able to operate cross-functionally, cross-divisionally, and cross-culturally around the world.

According to global management guru Kenichi Ohmae (1992), rule number one in globalization is "globalize people, globalize personnel." Since the process of globalization can take a long time, Ohmae emphasizes that companies should develop global people early. The number one priority is people: "You may have strategy, you may have visions, but unless you have global people, you can't deliver" (p. 28).

STEP 4: CONNECT GLOBAL TEAMS TO BUSINESS STRATEGIES AND OPERATIONS

The next step is to link—clearly and explicitly—all strategies and operations with the use of global teams. Strategic planning, manufacturing, marketing, distribution, R&D, customer service, administration, policy and procedures, technology acquisition and use—all should be undertaken with a mentality bent toward how global teams might contribute to further globalization and success of the enterprise. Ward (1999) suggests the following actions:

- Link the purpose of each global team to corporate strategic intent.
- Be clear about the key focus of the global team—be it global efficiency, local responsiveness, or organizational learning.
- Make huge increases in up-front investment of time, money, training, and technology to bring teams up to speed.

At regular intervals, the global teams should be assessed to determine the degree to which they have been globalized as well as the degree to which they have contributed to the globalization of the entire organization.

BP LEVERAGES GLOBAL TEAMS FOR ORGANIZATIONAL KNOWLEDGE AND SUCCESS

John Browne, CEO of BP, is a strong proponent of global teams as a key driver for the company's success. He firmly believes that every time a BP team does something, "it should do it better than the last time." He also recognizes that "knowledge is one of BP's most important assets and potentially its greatest source of competitive advantage." Thus he expects global teams to continuously assess how well they are helping the organization achieve its strategic objectives, what knowledge they are producing, and how their experiences can be converted into learning for BP.

STEP 5: RESTRUCTURE THE ORGANIZATION

As Ward (1999) notes, organizations must also recognize that they cannot simply create global teams in a vacuum and assume that everything else will remain the same. The birth of a global team will bring into sharp focus the way an organization operates—and can "act as a catalyst for a fundamental review of all organizational practices" (p. 13).

Bartlett and Ghoshal (1998) observe: "Perhaps the most important requirement for facilitating innovations is that the organizational configurations be based on a principle of reciprocal dependence among units. Such an interdependence of resources and responsibilities breaks down the hierarchy between local and global interests by making the sharing of resources, ideas and opportunities a self-enforcing norm" (pp. 128–129).

The challenge of top management is to look across an entire global enterprise and construct a configuration of teams that supports cross-cultural and cross-functional learning and innovation throughout the organization without interfering with local activities. This requires a systematic distribution of assets, resources, knowledge, skills, tasks, and responsibilities—all organized within the team context.

Global leaders need a clear understanding of the strengths and weaknesses of each business unit throughout the global network—and how they function together. This means "understanding how teams are best deployed for various strategic or tactical purposes and what kinds of technological support they need" (Devereaux and Johansen, 1994, p. 140).

Thus to fully support global teams, the organization needs to be restructured. A careful examination of what should be centralized and decentralized needs to be undertaken. Vertical and horizontal barriers must be eliminated. Functional activities may need to be welded into a seamless whole. Structures should be formed that allow for quick and accurate communications. Mechanisms that favor a single national culture must be dismantled.

Structures should be created that maximize worldwide operations and functions and enhance global universality while allowing for local diversity. The business dimension of global linking and leveraging must be stronger than geographic or functional dimensions. An integrated global strategy means integration across businesses within each country as well as integration within each business across countries. The organization has to transform itself into a team-based organization. And finally, the new organizational structure must be an enabling structure, not a barrier.

There are five major obstacles hindering the globalization process:

- *Bureaucracy*—where policies, regulations, forms, and busywork are more important than change

- *Competitiveness*—which emphasizes individuals rather than teams, teamwork, and collaboration

- *Control*—which may be exciting for those in control but hinders the delegation of power to global teams

- *Poor communication*—as a result of all the filters, biases, narrow listening, and delays

- *Rigid hierarchy*—which forces people and ideas to go up and down narrow silos

Royal Bank of Canada was one of the first companies in the world to simplify structures, eliminate silly rules and policies, and develop an organizationwide communication system that facilitates the success of its global teams. Global teams, as a result, function with a minimum of bureaucracy and a maximum of results and learning at this company.

STEP 6: DEVELOP POLICIES AND PRACTICES THAT SUPPORT GLOBAL TEAMS

As we've noted throughout this book, the organization must be prepared to provide a vast amount of support to its global teams—from the time of their creation to the completion of their projects. Organizations frequently underestimate the level and types of support needed by global teams. Here are some ways in which the organization can support its teams:

- Facilitate headquarters/subsidiary interactions.
- Create a supportive infrastructure.

- Implement team-friendly policies and practices in terms of HR, facilities, and technology.

- Involve key people up front—especially HR and information technology—on how these global teams can best be staffed, supported, facilitated, and trained.

- Be clear on the responsibilities of team sponsors, leaders, members, and facilitators.

- Provide training and support relative to cultural differences and synergies.

- Use visual tools to create mental models for cross-cultural work, including the use of a common language. This is why informational graphics—using visual imagery for communication—has become such a basic business tool for global teams.

The organization must be sure that the global team has the technical expertise to accomplish its tasks and the ability to secure team members from around the globe. It must also be sure to manage the team's organizational context and ensure that key sponsors and resource managers are kept well informed of the status of the global teams they interact with.

Organizations must find the opportunities inherent in the distance and time barriers of global teams rather than just seeing them as problems. For example: Can global teams provide freeways through the old boundaries of the organization so that widely dispersed members are able to conduct business around the clock? What's more, the rich cultural diversity of global teams means that multiple perspectives and insights are brought to bear in the search for innovation.

Ward (1999) cites three organizational factors that have a significant impact on the ultimate success of global teams for any organization:

- Respect of all the different cultures within the organization

- Wide geographic spread of the team members

- Integration of all the functional, professional, and other subcultures within the organization

ORGANIZATIONAL SUPPORT FOR GLOBAL TEAMS AT ALCOA

Mary Tomasello, HR Manager

In the early 1990s, as the number of plant locations continued to increase, the leaders of Alcoa's Primary Metals Business Unit were challenged with improving the speed and processes of the technology transfer system. A Technology Lead Team (TLT), sponsored by the Primary Metals Business Unit president and the director of operations, was formed to create a "technology family" of all the nine smelting locations in the United States, Brazil, and Australia.

Global teams were formed to determine how to best transfer technology throughout the nine plants. These teams are composed of members who are "close to the floor," such as pot room superintendents and electrode superintendents. Each has strong backing from business unit presidents as well as strong support from the highest levels of Alcoa. It is this sponsorship, commitment, and empowerment that has helped to reduce "work silos" and enables organizational members to communicate, perform, and learn more effectively and faster.

The main focus of the global teams continues to be on (1) identifying performance gaps, (2) performing internal and external benchmarking activities, (3) communicating best practices, and (4) making recommendations for process improvements and R&D.

As a result of the global team effort, the worldwide technological system continues to be leveraged with the sharing of financial and HR talent and the reduction of R&D costs. Such initiatives from the global teams have led to an increase in efficiency from 2 percent to 94 percent over a three-year period, an 80 percent reduction in the number of anode effects (emission of greenhouse gases), an increase of pot life, and a reduction of energy consumption.

In a recent interview, Jerry Roddy, one global leader, stated:

The keys to the success were strong sponsorship and a very clear mission. I would recommend to other groups who are interested in forming similar global teams to make sure they have sponsorship at both the business unit and location level. Both levels of sponsorship are important. In the beginning, when getting started, the business unit is most important. For the long term, however, the location managers, who control the plant resources, become more important. Corporate support and sponsorship have given the global teams the credibility needed to sustain long-term progress.

STEP 7: COMMIT THE HR UNIT TO SUPPORT GLOBAL TEAMS

Scott Snell et al. (1998) cite several key ways in which a company's HR unit can help in the creation and support of global teams: viewing the HR group as a model global team, developing a worldwide staffing network for future teams, providing team training as well as individual training, recognizing that many global teams are virtual teams, and reevaluating the career development system. Let's consider these suggestions one by one.

View the HR Group as a Model Global Team

The HR department generally has both corporate and local offices—subunits that must work together to establish an integrated whole despite their competing demands and responsibilities. This dual orientation within the HR group requires it to be a global team. At Glaxo-Wellcome, for example, the corporate HR group found that it had to undergo a team development process itself before it could effectively assist other global teams in the company. The Glaxo-Wellcome team formulated an HR strategy for facilitating team development in such areas as R&D and marketing. It also assembled a multinational team of process consultants to work with the teams.

Develop a Worldwide Staffing Network for Future Teams

To help provide staff for global teams, the HR department needs to adapt its information systems to establish the foundation for a worldwide staff network. The core of this network could be a computerized database containing information about global team candidates—including their work experience, previous performance, availability for team assignment, and skills.

Unilever, IBM, PricewaterhouseCoopers, and Colgate-Palmolive are examples of companies that have created sophisticated databases enabling the organization to identify potential team leaders and members. Their systems include candidates' personal preferences regarding types of and locations of global teams.

Provide Team Training as well as Individual Training

Training needs to be provided in three dimensions: (1) technical skills such as those required in project management and decision-making technologies; (2) team skills such as personal relations, conflict resolution, negotiations, and cultural sensitivity; and (3) company strategies, policies, and structures. The HR unit should provide some preliminary training before people are put on a global team. (Few companies have the luxury of waiting until after the team is formed to do all the necessary training.) The training should be delivered to intact teams as soon as possible—especially training in intercultural dynamics and group decision making. Without this kind of training, global teams may develop dysfunctional processes that are hard to correct later on.

Recognize That Many Global Teams Are Virtual Teams

Although most global team leaders and members may prefer to be co-located for ease of communication and decision making, in reality most global teams are virtual teams—that is, geographically dispersed. Thus they need to be held together by an ever-increasing array of interactive technologies. Global teams should be assured that they'll receive all the usual company training and support required by co-located teams as well as additional services because of their global status. These teams may need help in computer-based decision-support systems, management information systems, and planning and collaboration techniques.

Reevaluate the Career Development System

It is critically important for the HR unit to reassess the traditional career development system so that members of global teams are evaluated accurately and rewarded adequately. It also must evaluate global teams differently from national teams. What's more, global firms will need to reexamine the use of expatriates and consider three main alternatives to expatriation:

- More frequent short-term international assignments that do not involve high relocation costs
- More emphasis on the selection of new employees who already have some international experience
- More outsourcing and greater use of contingent workers

HR BUILDS GLOBAL TEAMS AND GLOBAL SUCCESS AT NOKIA

Pentti Sydanmaanlakka, HR Director

Human resources plays an important leadership role in promoting global teams and creating a truly global company. A global HR steering team composed of members from North America and Europe meets regularly and has assisted in the establishment of a number of global HR activities including:

- Global standard operating procedures for HR management
- A global HR Lotus Notes information system to enable global teams to share information more effectively
- Development of a global HR vision
- A global applicant tracking system and a global learning center network
- Active job rotation to truly globalize employees

STEP 8: PROVIDE GUIDELINES AND SUPPORT FOR DAY-TO-DAY OPERATIONS

Global groups, like any other group, go through a life cycle that requires solid organization support and involvement. Ward (1999) cites four phases of global teams and the key areas for corporate support:

Phase 1: Start-up Period Before the First Meeting

At this phase, it's important that team members are clear about their sponsors, their tasks, and their expected collaborations. Karen Ward recommends a "3 × 1" preparation. Thus if it takes one month to set up a co-located team, the company should plan on taking three months to set up a global team. And if a global team meeting is planned for one day, the company should plan on doing three days of preparation. Before the team begins to meet, the preparation should include:

- Determining the who, what, when, where, and how of key activities and processes

- Setting up informal and formal communication systems—critical for multicultural teams since incomplete communications may invite the wrong interpretation (and without ongoing feedback from trusted colleagues, the wrong explanation can be remembered for a long, long time)

- Ensuring round-the-clock accessibility to team leaders

- Defining a process for iterations and working on shared documents

- Setting goals—but letting teams fill in the specific steps in culturally acceptable ways and according to local conditions

- Setting milestones and reporting systems through the use of technology such as Lotus Notes

Phase 2: First Meeting

Apart from normal group process issues, Devereaux and Johansen (1994) emphasize that organizational leaders should encourage members of the new global team to learn each other's values about work, the meaning of collaboration, and the team's guiding principles. As discussed in Chapter 9, a key organizational resource is the presence of a facilitator to manage the global team's more complex interactions as well as its relationship with the rest of the organization. This person can also be invaluable in helping global teams develop processes for working effectively across great distances and time zones.

Phase 3: Midpoint

At the midpoint, the organization should assess the overall success of the team as well as process issues helped or hindered by cultural diversity, global distances, and technology.

Phase 4: Closing

In addition to evaluating the final results of the global team, the organization should make special efforts to ensure that the learning is passed on to other global teams of the company.

These four phases are cumulative: The better the cultural and organizational factors are planned and managed at each stage, the more productive and less troublesome the next phase will be. Conversely, the less corporate support the team gets and the more mistakes at the earlier stages, the more likely the global team will fail. There is no way to prepare for these areas specifically. You just have to be continually vigilant about such obstacles and develop contingency plans to deal with them effectively (Ward, 1999).

STEP 9: PROVIDE TECHNOLOGICAL SUPPORT

When providing technological support for the global teams, organizations should consider the following issues: selecting technologies, avoiding culturally biased technology, creating a technological network, cultivating nomadic technology brokers, ensuring security, and providing corporate training and support for use of technology.

Selecting Technologies

When determining appropriate communication technologies for use by global teams, the following points should be raised:

- *Availability:* To what extent are the various technologies available? Which technologies can be used regularly without putting anyone at a disadvantage?

- *User skills:* Is everyone adequately skilled with the different technology options?

- *Cultural variables:* Are these low-context or high-context cultures?

- *Level of rapport:* How well do we know each other?

- *Importance of the message:* Is the message of sufficient priority to dictate a high-context medium? Or will a low-context form of communication suffice?

- *Ways to build context:* Are there ways of creating richer context to enhance participation—such as in-person meetings, multiple media, and facilitation techniques?

- *Language modification:* When one language is used, are the native speakers considerate in their speech and transmission of written materials to non-native speakers?

For global teams, the simplest technologies (phone, fax, Internet, e-mail) may be the most valuable, at least in the short run. Devereaux and Johansen (1994) recommend focusing on the telephone—especially since the number of cellular phones is rapidly increasing globally and will soon surpass that of regular phones. (Finland averages more than one cell phone per person, for example.)

Avoiding Culturally Biased Technology

Although certain technologies may allow the organization to leap over great distances and time zones, they are generally incapable of crossing cultural boundaries. They may even be a hindrance since they are so strongly influenced by North American cultural values. Groupware will work only if it fits the user's culture. For example, technology that works in the United States (because it reflects American values of rationality, verifiability, efficiency, and productivity) is usually low in context and thus may not be so effective in high-context cultures.

The organization should therefore consider certain questions. Will a person from a visually oriented culture be more comfortable with video-teleconferencing than with audio? Is this comfort worth the cost? Do certain media have cultural meanings? Are certain topics easier to talk about or write about? Is translation needed? It's important to ask these questions at the beginning when it's much less expensive than having to switch technology later.

Given the various stages of global groups, some tasks require richer communication than others. Customer contact should be face-to-face when gathering requirements, for example, and later during prototyping. Designers need richer media to collaborate with one another during analysis and design phases. Any task requiring intense cooperation generally requires more communication—the richer the better. Conveying the vision to all cultures and groups, for example, must appeal to the emotional and motivational levels of all global team members.

When developing a global team communication strategy, the organization should also consider the amount of context available through different types of interaction. A person-to-person contact, for example, covers a whole range of possible interactions—including informal contact (in the hallway outside a meeting), a physical exchange (handshake or bow), nonverbal cues (facial expressions, gestures), immediate feedback, and voice tone.

Creating a Technological Network

Since communication is absolutely essential to global teams, it's critical to create the technological network that provides it. The Internet has made e-mail ubiquitous. In fact, e-mail is the backbone for global teams since it allows for different round-the-clock interactions regardless of time zone. Because of its written nature, moreover, e-mail is less likely to be misunderstood. What's more, graphics, images, and embedded programs can be exchanged at any time. E-mail systems allow a number of workflow-related programs to piggyback—group scheduling, project management, resource management tools, all essential for group coordination. Computer conferencing allows people to continue relationships they may have initiated on overseas visits. Videoconferencing, however, should be considered with caution as it may be unnecessary, too expensive, and inconvenient.

Cultivating Nomadic Technology Brokers

Devereaux and Johansen (1994) suggest that organizations consider the use of "nomadic technology brokers"—troubleshooters who not only ensure the proper functioning of their worldwide technology but also help global teams deal with bureaucratic and legal differences between countries and companies.

Ensuring Security

Wireless communications are certainly subject to eavesdropping. Thus companies must develop safeguards so that the global team can be confident its communications are private.

Providing Corporate Training and Support for Technology

Global teams may need a great deal of training and support to ensure that the appropriate technology is used well—particularly as it becomes more complex in function and integration. The company should also help global teams to become familiar with technology. (Many of us still suffer from technophobia.) It's important to recognize too that the extensive use of technology has redefined work itself. Thus support is required so that team members understand these new work processes and learn how to incorporate them into their team activities (Marquardt and Kearsley, 1999).

Devereaux and Johansen (1994) urge a final caution relative to technology: Many of the human, cultural, and organizational challenges of global teams are more amenable to human sensitivity than to technical solutions. Hence what is required is a top-priority, long-term, enterprise-wide commitment to continuous learning in the realms of culture, work process, and technology.

STEP 10: PROVIDE FAMILY SUPPORT

An important and frequent activity of global team members is traveling—with all of its joys as well as its frustrations. Organizations must remember that travel can create great emotional costs for the itinerant global worker. Team members who travel a lot may be lonely and suffer from low morale and deep fatigue. Thus every global worker needs to "calibrate his or her own tolerance level, because effectiveness diminishes rapidly when that level is passed" (Devereaux and Johansen, 1994, p. 143). For those on the road, keeping up morale and a sense of community is challenging. The organization should help its global team members create an upbeat atmosphere while traveling and allow both for compression and decompression time at either end of global meetings.

Before determining whether travel is necessary, two key questions should be asked:

- Are there trust issues to be worked out? If the team is in the early phase of formation and members represent a mix of high-context and low-context cultures, travel expenses may well be justified to resolve the tough issues of trust and team orientation.
- Does the problem involve highly sensitive cultural differences that cannot be resolved electronically?

Organizations should recognize the importance of easy access among partners on a global team. Dispersed members should have at least as much access to one another as colleagues at home and be able to respond quickly to emergencies. Travel protocols and norms should be established up front. The company must also provide a range of satisfying options between round-the-clock access to other team members and the organization, on the one hand, and a member's personal need for privacy on the other.

Finally, the organization must remember that global team members are usually working for more than one team and one supervisor. Conflicts can easily arise unless there are strong communications, shared priorities, and operating rules among company managers. Make sure that all teams are working in a common direction with a clear understanding of their place in the overall enterprise.

STEP 11: OPTIMIZE THE LEARNING AND SHARE IT

Since the importance and use of global teams will continue to grow, organizations should be sure to learn all the lessons from global teams—both the successful and the unsuccessful experiences. In fact, many companies rank organizational learning among the top reasons for establishing and supporting global teams (Marquardt, 1999; Nonaka and Takeuchi, 1995).

But for such learning to occur, a firm must develop operational systems that encourage team members to take the time to reflect on what has happened and why. Appraisal and reward systems must support learning that leads to innovation and new knowledge rather than focusing on short-term operational targets. Despite the importance of organizational learning as a strategic objective, Snell et al. (1998) note that few companies seem to make the effort.

STEP 12: CELEBRATE SUCCESSES AND ANCHOR GLOBAL TEAMS

It takes time, money, and much effort to build effective and successful global teams. Thus it's important to acknowledge the hurdles and challenges that have been overcome. As John Kotter (1996) has noted, the building of global teams, like any change effort, risks losing momentum if there are no short-term achievements to celebrate. Most people won't stay on the long march unless the journey has its milestones and short-term successes. Creating short-term wins is different from just hoping for them. Company leaders should look for ways to achieve and measure clear successes due to the activities of global teams.

Companies with successful teams should use the confidence gained from short-term victories to tackle even bigger problems. This is the time to confront systems and structures that are not consistent with the new vision.

SUCCESS WITH HIGH-PERFORMING GLOBAL TEAMS

The building of global teams is, indeed, the most important business challenge of the twenty-first century. Global success is now impossible without such teams. Their performance and power are now being seen by leaders worldwide as the key to competitiveness, productivity, and ultimate success in the network-style global organization of this new millennium.

Building global teams, however, requires a firm commitment and a well-orchestrated plan on the part of many people in the organization. Maintaining these successful global teams is an equally demanding challenge—one that requires a serious determination not to accept less than a high-quality, high-performing global team. We hope this book will provide the framework and guidelines that enable your global teams to become world-class teams.

A p p e n d i x   A

GlobalTeams Capability and Readiness Profile

The GlobalTeams Capability and Readiness Profile measures nine dimensions of team effectiveness: (1) Effective Leadership for Global Teams, (2) Creating a Challenging Vision and a Shared Team Identity, (3) Building Swift Trust and Strong Norms, (4) Cultural Diversity and Global Integration, (5) Technological Support and Communications, (6) Harnessing Cultural, Interpersonal and Technical Expertise, (7) Global Team Facilitation, (8) Measurement and Feedback Systems, and (9) Team-Oriented Assessment and Rewards.

This survey is designed to give global teams information about each of these components and hence offer guidance for improved team functioning. We suggest that the instrument be completed and reviewed by team members and also by key team constituents (customers, managers, colleagues). The strengths and weaknesses identified through this instrument can serve as a foundation. Not only will they indicate the capability of your team, but they point out the steps that can be taken to improve each of the nine global team dimensions.

The survey consists of a list of fifty statements about your team. Read each statement carefully and decide the extent to which it applies to your team. Use the following scale:

4 = applies totally

3 = applies to a great extent

2 = applies to a moderate extent

1 = applies to little or no extent

GLOBAL TEAMS

1. Team Leadership

In this team:

____ Team leadership is aware of developments and events outside the team that affect the team's mission and operations.

____ Team leadership keeps the team aligned with the organization's strategy and operations.

____ The team leader communicates organizational goals so they are clear to all team members.

____ Team leadership obtains input on how to align the team's strategy with the goals.

____ The team leader uses the cultural diversity of the team members for creative solutions.

____ The team leader is committed to achieving consensus on work and communication styles and keeping all team members involved.

| TOTAL SCORE

2. Team Vision and Identity

In this team:

____ The team charter and mission statement reflect the team vision.

____ The team vision is translated into long-term strategies, shorter-term operational tactics, and goals, plans, and tasks.

____ The team vision is developed through a collaborative process with team members.

____ The key strategic focus of the team (efficiency, local responsiveness, organizational learning) is linked to the organization's strategic intent and is communicated to team members.

____ The team mission is depicted in key words and simple graphics that are understood and accepted by many cultures.

____ Our identity as a team is shaped by our vision, mission, and values.

| TOTAL SCORE

3. Swift Trust and Strong Norms

In this team:

____ Trust is demonstrated through bargaining, testing, and reflection.

____ Regular communication and time for bonding are a priority.

____ Members rely on one another to achieve team goals.

____ Members are alert, knowledgeable, and accepting of cultural differences.

____ Disciplined work processes and norms are outlined at the creation of the team and are carried out.

____ We have confidence in each other's competence and efforts.

[ ] TOTAL SCORE

4. Cultural Diversity and Global Integration

In this team:

____ We recognize the value and power of cultural diversity.

____ Group members have been trained in working with people of other cultures.

____ Positive mutual attitudes among cultural groups prevail, and there is no status difference among cultures.

____ A global mind-set is shared so that we see the world without boundaries or cultural bias.

____ Global issues of cultural sensitivity, respect, timeliness, and worklife quality are valued.

____ The impact of culture on leadership, decision making, and communication is understood.

[ ] TOTAL SCORE

5. Technological Support and Communications

In this team:

___ Team needs and team processes are determined first—then the appropriate technology is applied.

___ We understand the technologies available for information, for decision making, and for learning.

___ Technological vendors and products are always checked for cultural appropriateness and compatibility.

___ Team members and constituents are involved in the design of the technological systems.

___ Team members agree on a common means of communication.

☐ TOTAL SCORE

6. Cultural, Interpersonal, and Technical Expertise

In this team:

___ Members are selected on the basis of gaining diverse perspectives and their ability to achieve the organization's goals for the team.

___ Training is aligned with the overall tasks and mission of the team.

___ Training is given on cross-cultural awareness and conflict resolution skills.

___ Development of skills in reaching consensus is highly valued.

___ The training context is designed to be flexible so that members can learn and develop individually and as a team.

___ Training is given throughout the life cycle of the team.

☐ TOTAL SCORE

7. Global Team Facilitation

In this team:

____ We use a facilitator to help us document problems that arise in the team discussions.

____ The facilitator helps the team learn from personal and group interactions.

____ The facilitator concentrates his or her efforts at the design as well as the implementation stages.

____ The facilitator builds consensus about how to surmount cultural differences over team objectives, processes, leadership styles, and status of individual members.

____ The facilitator encourages the team to reach consensus on how to accommodate differing degrees of fluency (spoken and written) in the common language for doing business.

☐ TOTAL SCORE

8. Measurement and Feedback Systems

In this team:

____ The measurement system incorporates the organization's business strategy and is clear to team members.

____ Measures relate to the team's tasks, time, location, composition, and levels of experience.

____ Team members share in designing the measurement systems.

____ Measurement systems are continually reviewed by management so that they are capturing elements essential to the team goals.

____ Measurement feedback is presented in order to solve problems rather than evaluate individual performance.

☐ TOTAL SCORE

GLOBAL TEAMS

9. Appraisal and Rewards

In this team:

_____ Individual, team, and home country rewards are combined into reward systems.

_____ Compensation and appraisal of individual team members are relevant to their home-based workplaces.

_____ Evaluations are done by home country managers with input from team leaders and members.

_____ Team members are involved in devising the appraisal and compensation systems.

_____ The team compensation and appraisal systems are specific, equitable, timely, and communicated clearly.

[ ] TOTAL SCORE

SCORING KEY

[ ] TOTAL SCORE FOR NINE DIMENSIONS OF GLOBAL TEAMS

161–200 Congratulations! You are well on your way to becoming a strong and effective global team.

121–160 Keep on moving! Your global team has a solid foundation.

81–120 A good beginning! Your global team has gathered some important building blocks.

80 or Below Watch out! Time to make drastic changes if you want to survive as a global team.

Appendix B

Web Sites on Global Teams

High-Performance Team
http://rampages.onramp.net/~bodwell/home.html
Issues related to high-performance teams including team building and coaching

Self-Directed Work Teams Page
http://users.ids.net/~brim/
Information related to self-directed work teams including books, videos, bibliographies

Team Management Systems
http://www.tms.com.au/welcome.html
Comprehensive sites with research, discussion forum, case studies/ articles, news, links

Wings Group: TeamZene
http://www.maine.com/wings/Teamzene_past.html
Articles on teaming issues; free e-magazine

Team Technology
http://www.teamtechnology.co.uk/tt/index.html
Information on team building and links to related sites

Teambuilding, Inc.
http://www.teambuildinginc.com/
Information on employee involvement including discussion area, articles, links

GLOBAL TEAMS

Orient Pacific Century
http://www.orientpacific.com/opcteam.html
Information on team building focused on the Asian context, strategic and market research

The Networking Institute
http://www.netage.com/
Information focused on virtual teams including research, articles, current events, links

CORE—R.O.I., Inc.
http://COREROI.COM/publica.htm
Information on team-building-related links

Involve—Free Web Teaming
http://www.involv.net/
Free interactive site for teams and groups

TeamTrac, Inc.
http://www.teamtrac.com/
Team-building information including tips, articles, references, surveys

Stages of Team Development
http://dspace.dial.pipex.com/town/estate/dd75/teamwork/tsld005.html
Information on team development model

Teams and Teamwork
http://www.hq.nasa.gov/office/hqlibrary/ppm/ppm5.htm
NASA team site

Well-Functioning Group
http://www.virtualschool.edu/98c/Soci305/Soci305Miller.html
Case study

Glenn Parker's Website
http://www.glennparker.com/Information/about-glenn-parker.html
Team-building information including exercises, articles, icebreakers, tips

APPENDIX B

TEAM Management Systems
http://www.tms.com.au/tms04.html
Information on team management including case studies and newsletter

Center for Quality of Management
http://www.cqm.org/
Comprehensive site on integration, implementation, and diffusion of best management practices related to quality

Center for the Study of Work Teams
http://www.workteams.unt.edu/
Comprehensive site with links, research, articles, newsletter

Roger Schwarz & Associates
http://www.schwarzassociates.com/
Site dedicated to group facilitation information including training, links, resources

Resources for Meeting and Group Process
http://www.infoteam.com/nonprofit/nica/meeting.html
Comprehensive listing of links, books, articles

Center for Group Learning
http://www.cgl.org/
Listing of group tools, information, organizations

Center for the Study of Group Processes
http://www.uiowa.edu/~grpproc/
Information on group process including research, events, links

Virtual Organization Research Network
http://www.virtual-organization.net/
Contains e-journal, e-news, articles, links

Virtual Organization
http://www.seanet.com/~daveg/articles.html
Information on virtual organizations including articles and surveys

Journal of Computer-Mediated Communication
http://www.ascusc.org/jcmc/vol3/issue4/
Special issue on virtual organizations

CSCW Bibliography
http://www.telekooperation.de/cscw/cscw-biblio.html
Contains articles on computer-supported communicated work

Managing Virtual Teams
http://www.tmn.com/~lisa/vteams-toronto.htm
Speech on virtual teams given by Lisa Kimball for Team Strategies Conference

References

Abdullah, A. 1996. *Going global.* Kuala Lumpur: MIM Press.

Allen, T. 1997. *Managing the flow of technology.* Cambridge, MA: MIT Press.

Apte, U., and R. Mason. 1995. Global disintegration of information-intensive services. *Management Science* 41, no. 7: 1250–1262.

Ashforth, B., and F. Mael. 1989. Social identity theory and the organization. *Academy of Management Review* 4, no. 1: 20–39.

Baker, D. P., and E. Salas. 1997. Principles for measuring teamwork: A summary and look toward the future. In M. T. Brannick and E. Salas (eds.), *Team performance assessment and measurement: Theory, methods, and applications.* Hillsdale, NJ: Erlbaum.

Bartlett, C., and S. Ghoshal. 1998. *Managing across borders.* Boston: Harvard Business School Press.

Bartol, L., and L. Hagmann. 1992. Team-based pay plans: A key to effective teamwork. *Compensation & Benefits Review* 24, no. 6: 24–29.

Berger, M. 1996a. *Cross-cultural team building: Guidelines for more effective communication and negotiation.* London: McGraw-Hill.

Berger, M. 1996b. Introduction to cross-cultural team building. In M. Berger (ed.), *Cross-cultural team building: Guidelines for more effective communication and negotiation.* London: McGraw-Hill.

Berger, M. 1996c. Facilitation skills for cross-cultural team building. In M. Berger (ed.), *Cross-cultural team building: Guidelines for more effective communication and negotiation.* London: McGraw-Hill.

Bikson, T. K., S. G. Cohen, and D. Mankin. 1999. Information technology and high-performance teams. In E. Sundstrom and Associates (eds.), *Supporting work team effectiveness.* San Francisco: Jossey-Bass.

Brannick, M. T., and C. Prince. 1997. An overview of team performance measurement. In M. T. Brannick and E. Salas (eds.), *Team performance assessment and measurement: Theory, methods, and applications.* Hillsdale, NJ: Erlbaum.

Brannick, M. T. and E. Salas (eds.). 1997. *Team performance assessment and measurement: Theory, methods, and applications*. Hillsdale, NJ: Erlbaum.

Carmel, E. 1999. *Global software teams*. Upper Saddle River, NJ: Prentice-Hall.

Caudron, S. 1994. Tie individual pay to team success. *Personnel Journal* 73, no. 19: 40–46.

Clackworthy, D. 1996. Training Germans and Americans in conflict management. In M. Berger (ed.), *Cross-cultural team building: Guidelines for more effective communication and negotiation*. London: McGraw-Hill.

Davenport, T., and K. Prusa. 1998. *Working knowledge*. Cambridge, MA: Harvard Business School Press.

Davison, S. 1996. Leading and facilitating international teams. In M. Berger (ed.), *Cross-cultural team building: Guidelines for more effective communication and negotiation*. London: McGraw-Hill.

Davison, S., and K. Ward. 1999. *Leading international teams*. London: McGraw-Hill.

Devereaux, M., and R. Johansen. 1994. *GlobalWork: Bridging distance, culture, and time*. San Francisco: Jossey-Bass.

Dixon, N. 1998. Building global capacity with global task teams. *Performance Improvement Quarterly* 11, no. 1: 108–112.

Dutton, J., J. Dukerish, and C. Harquail. 1994. Organizational images and member identification. *Administrative Science Quarterly* 39, no. 2: 239–264.

Gross, S. E. 1995. *Compensation for teams: How to design and implement team-based reward systems*. New York: American Management Association.

Grove, C., and C. G. Hallowell. 1998. Spinning your wheels? Successful global teams know how to gain traction. *HR Magazine* 43, no. 5: 24–28.

Gundling, E. 1999. How to communicate globally. *Training and Development* 53, no. 6: 28–31.

Hackman, J. R., and R. E. Walton. 1986. Leading groups in organizations. In P. S. Goodman and Associates (eds.), *Designing effective work groups*. San Francisco: Jossey-Bass.

Hambrick, D. C., S. C. Davison, S. A. Snell, and C. A. Snow. 1998. When groups consist of multiple nationalities: Towards a new understanding of the implications. *Organization Studies* 19, no. 2: 181–205.

Hamel, G., and C. K. Prahalad. 1994. *Competing for the future*. Boston: Harvard Business School Press.

Hampden-Turner, D., and F. Trompenaars. 1997. *Mastering the infinite game: How East Asian values are transforming business practices*. New York: Business Book Network.

REFERENCES

Handy, C. 1995. *Trust and the virtual organization.* Harvard Business Review 73, no. 3: 40–50.

Heifetz, R., and D. Laurie. 1998. *Leadership: Mobilizing adaptive work.* Unpublished.

Hoffer, J. A., and J. S. Valacich. 1993. Group memory in group support systems: A foundation for design. In L. M. Jessup and J. S. Valacich (eds.), *Group support systems: New perspectives.* New York: Macmillan.

Hofstede, G. 1991. *Cultures and organizations.* London: McGraw-Hill.

Hogg, M. 1996. Identity, cognition and language in intergroup context. *Journal of Language and Social Psychology* 15, no. 3: 372–384.

Hosmer, L. T. 1995. Trust: The connecting link between organizational theory and philosophical ethics. *Academy of Management Journal* 20, no. 2: 379–403.

Jarvenpaa, S. L., K. Knoll, and D. E. Leidner. 1998. Is anybody out there? Antecedents of trust in global virtual teams. *Journal of Management Information Systems* 14, no. 4: 29–64.

Jones, S., and R. G. Moffett. 1999. Measurement and feedback systems for teams. In E. Sundstrom and Associates (eds.), *Supporting work team effectiveness.* San Francisco: Jossey-Bass.

Kingston, P. 1996. Bridging the language gap through international networking. In M. Berger (ed.), *Cross-cultural team building: Guidelines for more effective communication and negotiation.* London: McGraw-Hill.

Klimoski, R. J., and L. B. Zukin. 1999. Selection and staffing for team effectiveness. In E. Sundstrom and Associates (eds.), *Supporting work team effectiveness.* San Francisco: Jossey-Bass.

Kotter, J. 1996. *Leading change.* Boston: Harvard Business School Press.

Lawler, E. E. 1999. Creating effective pay systems for teams. In E. Sundstrom and Associates (eds.), *Supporting work team effectiveness.* San Francisco: Jossey-Bass.

LeBoeuf, M. 1985. *The greatest management principle in the world.* Berkeley: Berkeley Publishing.

Lee, A. 1997. *Team compensation: A broad overview.* Denton, TX: CSWT Reports.

Marmer, C. 1995. Global teams: The ultimate collaboration. *Personnel Journal* 74, no. 9: 1–49.

Marquardt, M. 1996. *Building the learning organization.* New York: McGraw-Hill.

Marquardt, M. 1999. *The global advantage: How world-class organizations improve performance through globalization.* Houston: Gulf Press.

Marquardt, M., and D. Engel. 1993. *Global human resource development*. Englewood Cliffs, NJ: Prentice-Hall.

Marquardt, M., and G. Kearsley. 1999. *Technology-based learning*. Boca Raton, FL: St. Lucie Press.

Marquardt, M., and A. Reynolds. 1994. *The global learning organization*. Burr Ridge, IL: Irwin.

McDermott, L. C., B. Nolan, and W. Waite. 1998. *World class teams: Working across borders*. New York: Wiley.

McGrath, J. E. 1962. *Leadership behavior: Some requirements for leadership training*. Washington, DC: Civil Service Commission.

McShulskis, E. 1996. Global teams popular, but difficult. *HR Magazine* 41, no. 12: 18–19.

Mendenhall, M., and G. Oddou. 1998. The overseas assignment: A practical look. *Business Horizons* (Sept.–Oct.): 78–84.

Mittleman, D., and R. Briggs. 1999. Communication technologies for traditional and virtual teams. In E. Sundstrom and Associates (eds.), *Supporting work team effectiveness*. San Francisco: Jossey-Bass.

Niehoff, B., C. Enz, and R. Grover. 1990. The impact of top-management actions on employee attitudes and perceptions. *Group and Organizational Studies* 15, no. 3: 337–453.

Nonaka, I., and H. Takeuchi. 1996. *The knowledge-creating company*. New York: Oxford University Press.

Oddou, G., and M. Mendenhall. 1988. *Cases in international organizational behaviour*. Cambridge, England: Blackwell.

Ohmae, K. 1992. *The borderless world*. New York: Harperbusiness.

Peters, T. 1992. *Liberation management*. New York: Knopf.

Rhinesmith, S. 1996. *Globalization: Six keys to success in a changing world*. New York: McGraw-Hill.

Schwandt, D., and M. Marquardt. 2000. *Organizational learning: From world-class theories to global best practices*. Boca Raton, FL: St. Lucie Press.

Schwarz, R. M. 1994. *The skilled facilitator: Practical wisdom for developing effective groups*. San Francisco: Jossey-Bass.

Sheehan, T., and K. Murray. 1990. The art of training abroad. *Training and Development Journal* 44, no. 1: 15–18.

Smolek, J., D. Hoffman, and L. Moran. 1999. Organizing for team effectiveness. In E. Sundstrom and Associates (eds.), *Supporting work team effectiveness*. San Francisco: Jossey-Bass.

Snell, S., C. Snow, S. Davison, and D. C. Hambrick. 1998. Designing and supporting transitional teams: The human resource agenda. *Human Resource Management* 37, no. 2: 147–148.

REFERENCES

Snow, C., S. A. Snell, S. C. Davison, and D. C. Hambrick. 1996. Use transnational teams to globalize your company. *Organizational Dynamics* 24, no. 4: 50–68.

Stepanek, M. 1999. Using the net for brainstorming: Smart companies are exploiting the cyberspace to spark innovation. *Business Week,* Dec. 13, pp. 55–60.

Stevens, M. J., and M. E. Yarish. 1999. Training for team effectiveness. In E. Sundstrom and Associates (eds.), *Supporting work team effectiveness.* San Francisco: Jossey-Bass.

Stewart, T. 1997. *Intellectual capital.* New York: Doubleday.

Storti, C. 1991. *The art of crossing cultures.* Yarmouth, ME: Intercultural Press.

Sundstrom, E. 1999. The challenges of supporting work team effectiveness. In E. Sundstrom and Associates (eds.), *Supporting work team effectiveness.* San Francisco: Jossey-Bass.

Sundstrom, E., and Associates. 1999. *Supporting work team effectiveness.* San Francisco: Jossey-Bass.

Sveiby, K. 1997. *The new organizational wealth.* San Francisco: Berrett-Koehler.

Tjosvold, D., and Y. Tsao. 1989. Productive organizational collaboration: The roles of values and cooperation. *Journal of Organizational Behavior* 10, no. 2: 189–196.

Trompenaars, F. 1994. *Riding the waves of culture.* New York: McGraw-Hill.

Van Houten, G. 1990. Managing human resources in the international firm. In P. Evans, Y. Doz, and A. Laurent (eds.), *Human resources management in international firms: Change, globalization, and innovation.* New York: St. Martin's Press.

Wageman, R. 1997. Critical success factors for creating superb self-managing teams. *Organizational Dynamics* 26, no. 1: 49–61.

Ward, K. 1999. International teams: Do you have what it takes? *Directions* (July): 12–19.

Young, D. 1998a. Field of teams. *CIO* 11, no. 22: 22–24.

Young, D. 1998b. Team heat. *CIO* 11, no. 22: 42–51.

Zaccaro, S. J., and M. A. Marks. 1999. The roles of leaders in high-perfor-mance teams. In E. Sundstrom and Associates (eds.), *Supporting work team effectiveness.* San Francisco: Jossey-Bass.

Index

acculturation, 167
adaptive problems, 9–10
Allen, Thomas, 29
alliances, 16–17
anticipation, 25
appraisal systems. *See* performance appraisals

benefits: alliance forming, 16–17; cost reductions, 7–8; customer relations, 13–14; economies of scope, 7–8; efficiency, 77; globalization of company, 11–12; knowledge and information access, 15–16; leader development, 14–15; learning organization focus, 17; local response, 77; problem solving, 9–11; specialized talent, 9; speed of operations, 12–13
boundaries, 36–37
building of global teams: barriers, 210; commitment to, 204–205; company examples of, 205–206, 212–213; corporate culture that supports, 207; day-to-day operations guidelines and support, 215–217; family support, 220–221; human resources commitment, 213–215; learning in organization, 221–222; linkage to business strategies and operations, 208; organization support for, 210–211; organization's readiness assessed, 206–207; overview of, 222; policies and programs to support, 210–213; restructuring of organization, 209–210; sense of urgency for, 204–205; successes celebrated, 222; technological support, 217–220
buy-in, 189

cable TV, 134
career development system, 214–215
CD-ROM, 134
challenges: assessment of, 39–40; communication, 30–33; control, 29–30; coordination, 29–30; cultural diversity, 20–27. *See also* cultural diversity; description of, 18–19; geographic distance, 27–29; overcoming of, 36–38, 203–204; team maintenance and development, 33–34

charter, 72–74, 88–89
chat systems, 122
collaborative writing systems, 122
communication: company examples of, 52, 91–93, 106–107; context of, 30–32; cultural influences, 22–24, 105–106; electronic methods of, 76, 123–128; e-mail, 106–107, 121, 124–125; expressive style of, 22–23, 105; face-to-face, 93, 163; facilitator, 167, 171–172; flexibility in, 62; geographic distance effects, 28–29; globalization effects, 210; in high-context culture, 30–31, 33, 105; importance of, 90–91; indirect, 24–25; instrumental style of, 23, 105; in low-context culture, 31–33, 105; methods of, 76, 123–128; nonverbal, 31–32; team members, 90–91, 138–139; trust building and, 90–91, 93
compensation system: challenges associated with, 198–199; designing of, 194, 198–199; flexibility of, 200; guidelines for, 199–201; local market considerations, 201; team-specific considerations, 194. *See also* reward system
competitive cultures, 26, 112–113
computer-based training, 133
conflict resolution: cultural influences, 24–25; training, 148–149
continuous learning, 116
control: definition of, 29; globalization effects, 210
controlled culture, 23
cooperative culture, 26–27, 112–113
coordination: definition of, 29; interdependence effects, 30
correspondence, 25
cost reductions, 7–8
courage building, 63
covert revelation, 25
cross-cultural training, 60, 62, 102, 149–150
cultural customization, 116
cultural diversity: communication, 105–106; company example of, 113–115; competitive vs. cooperative culture, 112–113; description of, 20; facilitator's role in understanding, 162–163, 165, 171; global integration and, 116–117; groupings, 103–104; language considerations, 107–109; leadership effects, 49, 51–58; synergized view of, 118; team effects, 34; tips for managing, 104, 118; training based on, 151–154; unification of team, 115–117; valuing of, 102–103
cultural empathy, 167–168
cultural knowledge, 60
cultural learning: description of, 60, 94; importance of, 102; training methods, 60, 62
cultural norms, 53, 62, 162
cultural sensitivity, 94, 116
culture: communication styles, 22–23, 105–106; company examples of, 35–36, 113–115; competitive, 26, 112–113; conflict management based on, 24–25; controlled, 23; cooperative, 26–27, 112–113; decision-making approaches, 24; definition of, 20, 101; differences,

INDEX

20–21, 27; disagreements, 24–25; facilitator's knowledge and appreciation of, 165–166; feedback and, 163; flexibility, 26, 166–167; future-oriented, 26; grouping of members, 103–104; hierarchy considerations, 103–104; high-context, 30–31, 105, 188; in-control, 23; individualism, 22; influences of, 103; leadership roles and expectations, 21–22, 109; low-context, 31–32, 188; monochronic, 25; motivation, 26–27; particularistic, 23; performance appraisal considerations, 197; polychronic, 25–26; present-focused, 26; problem-solving approaches based on, 23, 111–112; punctuality attitudes, 25, 110; time differences, 25–26, 110; tradition-based, 26; universalistic, 23; vision acceptance of, 77
customers, 13–14

databases, 131–132
data-gathering skill, 61
decision making: cultural influences, 24; skills in, 61
definition, 4
diagnosis skill, 61, 164
direction setting: leader's role in, 48, 50, 53, 59; vision for, 68
distribution technologies, 134–135
documentation, 43

economies of scope, 7–8
educational system, 49
electronic publishing, 133

e-mail, 106–107, 121, 124–125, 134, 219
empathy: cultural, 167–168; leader, 63–64
employee: geographic distance effects, 28; leadership development, 14–15. *See also* team members
envisioning skill, 61
EPSS, 134
ethnocentrism, 166
expatriation, 215
external linkages: cultural influences, 51; leader's role in managing, 47, 50, 59
extranet, 134
eye contact, 106

facilitation: acculturated, 167; company examples of, 172–176; definition of, 160; difficulties encountered, 162–163; guidelines for, 171–172; ongoing nature of, 160
facilitator(s): approach used by, 172; assessments of, 169–170; benefits of, 176–177; communication skills of, 167, 171–172; company examples of, 158–159, 172–176; cultural flexibility of, 166–167; cultural knowledge and sensitivity, 164–166, 171; empathy of, 167–168; function of, 161–162; global mind-set of, 166; importance of, 176–177, 216; learning commitment, 168; lessons learned, 172; multiple, 171; need for, 157–158, 160; and overcoming difficulties, 162–163; participation of, 160;

facilitator(s) *cont'd*
  phase-specific responsibilities of, 163, 171; roles of, 158, 160–161; sense of humor, 168; skills of, 164–170; values of, 161, 171
facsimile communication, 123
family support, 220–221
feedback system: company example of, 182–183; cultural considerations, 188; designing of, 179–183; elements necessary for creating, 179–180; facilitator's role, 163–165; future trends, 190; guidelines for, 185, 187, 189–190; need for, 181; productivity improvements as goal of, 180, 185; rewards and, 191; tailoring for global teams, 183–187; team participation in developing, 180, 184–185
flexibility: compensation system, 200; cultural, 166–167
focus groups, 146–147
forecasting skill, 61

geographic distance: challenges associated with, 27–29; communication effects, 28–29; employee morale effects, 28–29; problem solving effects, 28; teamness effects, 34
global facilitator. *See* facilitator(s)
global mind-set: developing of, 207; facilitator, 166; team members, 116
global teams: advantages of, 77; benefits. *See* benefits; building of. *See* building of global teams; characteristics of, 4–5; company examples of, 3–4, 8, 11–12; cultural diversity in. *See* cultural diversity; definition of, 4; interdependence, 30; management involvement in, 203; need for, 6; obstacles, 4; phases of, 215–217; power of, 6–7; size of, 30, 34; virtual nature of, 214; web sites, 229–232. *See also* team
globalization: barriers to, 210; benefits of, 11; creation of, 12, 115, 207; cultural diversity and, 116–117; description of, 5
GlobalTeams Capacity and Readiness Profile, 223–228
glocalized companies, 13
group calendars, 121
groupings, 103–104
groupware: asynchronous, 121–122; benefits of, 120; categorization of, 120; description of, 119–120; products, 126; synchronous, 122, 126–128

Handy, Charles, 28
hierarchy: culture and, 103–104; globalization effects, 210
high-context culture: characteristics of, 30–31, 105; feedback considerations, 188
human resources unit: career development system, 214–215; commitment of, 213–215; company example of, 215; policies and programs of, 38, 199; team member selection participation, 146, 213–214
hypertext, 121
hypothesis-testing skill, 61

ideas, 10
identity, 76

INDEX

implementation skill, 62
in-control culture, 23
individualism, 22
information: access to, 15–16; importance of, 15–16
information system, 49
information technology: team member involvement in implementing, 132; types of, 119–130; use of, 131–132. *See also* technology
interdependence, 30
Internet: advantages and disadvantages of, 125, 219; company example of, 132–133; definition of, 134
interpersonal skill, 62
interpretation skills, 164
intranet, 122, 134
inventive skill, 61

knowledge: access to, 15–16; global teams linked to organizational knowledge, 208; importance of, 15

language: cultural diversity in, 107–109; skills, 62; team member training, 149–150
leader: assessing performance of, 180; attributes of, 63–65; courage building, 63; cultural competency training, 60, 62; cultural differences that affect, 49, 51–58; development of, 14–15, 64, 151–152; difficulties of, 43–44; direction setting by, 48, 50, 53, 59; early-stage participation, 56–58; empathy of, 63–64; external linkages managed by, 47, 50, 59; liaison role of, 51; openness of, 63; operations management, 48–50, 59; resources acquisition, 49–50, 58–59; responsibilities of, 43; roles, 46–49; selection of, 146–147; skills of, 58, 60–62; team functioning effects, 55–56; Western vs. non-Western, 21–22
leadership: commitment of, 204–205; company example of, 45–46; cultural influences, 21–22, 55–56, 109–110; expectations of, 56–58; guidelines, 44–45, 64
learning: abilities to increase, 17; continuous, 116, 168; facilitator's commitment to, 168; organizational, 77, 199, 221–222; skill, 61; technologies for, 133–135
LeBoeuf, Michael, 191
local-area network, 134
low-context culture: characteristics of, 31–32; feedback considerations, 188

mailing lists, 121
management: challenges for, 209; commitment of, 204–205; involvement of, 203. *See also* leadership
measurement system: company example of, 182–183, 186–187; cultural considerations, 188; customer needs addressed in, 180; effectiveness-based, 184; elements necessary for, 179–180; future trends, 190; guidelines for, 185, 187, 189–190; human resources unit

measurement system, *cont'd*
    participation, 214; measures for assessing, 196; need for, 181; performance-based, 184; rewards and, 191; tailoring for global teams, 183–187; team participation in developing, 180, 184–185. *See also* performance appraisals
mediation, 25
meetings: cultural considerations in scheduling, 110; team members, 87–90, 216; virtual, 131
members. *See* team members
mind-set: developing of, 207; facilitator, 166; team members, 116
mission statement, 74–75
monochronic culture, 25
Morita, Akio, 102
motivation, cultural differences in, 26–27
multiculturalism, 102

negotiation skill, 61
networking, 47, 219
newsgroups, 121
nonverbal communication, 31–32

obstacles, 4, 210
Ohmae, Kenichi, 207
operations: leader's role in managing, 48–50; speed of, 12–13
organization: alliances with, 16–17; leader's role in acquiring support of, 49; learning in, 77, 199, 221–222; readiness of, 206–207; restructuring of, 209–210
orientation of team members, 87–90

particularistic culture, 23
pay. *See* compensation system
performance appraisals: company example of, 195, 201–202; cultural considerations, 197; guidelines, 195; learning supported by, 221; measures assessed, 196; outcomes-based, 196; rewards and, 194–195; steps recommended for, 200–201. *See also* measurement system
personnel. *See* team members
Peters, Tom, 5
polychronic culture, 25–26
pooled interdependence, 30
presentation technologies, 133–134
present-focused culture, 26
problem solving: adaptive, 9–10; company example of, 11; cultural influences, 23, 111–112; direction setting, 53; geographic distance effects, 28; technical, 9; technology for, 138
punctuality, 25, 110

reciprocal interdependence, 30
refraction, 25
representing, 47
resources: distribution of, 55; leader's role in acquiring, 49–50, 58
reward system: company example of, 201–202; description of, 49; feedback and, 191; goal of, 194; importance of, 193; learning supported by, 221; monetary vs. nonmonetary, 194; organizational learning, 199; performance effects, 194–195; team-based, 194. *See also* compensation system

INDEX

ritual, 25
Roddy, Jerry, 212–213

satellite TV, 135
sense making, 47
sense of humor, 168
sequential interdependence, 30
simulations, 132
simulator, 135
skill(s): cross-cultural, 62; data-gathering, 61; development of, 58, 60–62; diagnosis, 61, 164; envisioning, 61; facilitator, 164–170; feedback, 164–165; forecasting, 61; hypothesis-testing, 61; implementation, 62; interpersonal, 62; interpretation, 164; inventive, 61; language, 62; leader, 58, 60–62; learning, 61; measuring of, 182; negotiation, 61; teaching, 61; types of, 61–62
swift trust: company example of, 83–86; definition of, 82–83; guidelines for developing, 87–95; implementing of, 86–87; importance of building, 82–83; overview of, 97. *See also* trust

teaching skill, 61
team: boundaries in, 36–37; building of, 55; cohesiveness of, 34, 36, 115–116; cultural influences, 34; direction setting, 48, 50, 53, 59; future of, 5–6; importance of, 5; interdependence, 30; maintenance of, 33–34; self-management capacity of, 162; vision of. *See* vision of team. *See also* global teams
team facilitator. *See* facilitator(s)

team members: communication, 90–91, 138–139; company examples of, 143–144, 146; competencies, 145, 188; development of, 148–149; expectations of, 163; first meeting of, 87–90, 216; global mind-set of, 116, 207; grouping of, 103–104; information technology implementation, 132; language training, 149–150; measurement of. *See* feedback system, measurement system; orientation of, 87–90; part-time, 199; potential of, 55; satisfaction assessments, 57–58; selection of, 145–147, 213–214; training of, 148–149; trust building, 89–90
team outcomes, 180, 196
team process, 180–181
technical problems, 9
technology: benefits of, 120–121; communication, 9, 119–130; company examples of, 128–130, 135–137; contact available based on, 219; cultural considerations, 218–219; description of, 119; designing of, 138–139; effects of, 6; guidelines for, 138–139, 217–218; implementing of, 138–139; information, 119–130, 131–132; learning, 133–135; network, 219; nomadic brokers of, 219; security considerations, 220; selecting of, 217–218; support for, 220; training considerations, 220; use of, 130–131. *See also specific technology*
teleconference, 123, 134

time, cultural differences regarding, 25–26, 110
tradition-based culture, 26
training: company examples of, 152–154; computer-based, 133; cross-cultural, 60, 62, 102, 149–150; culturally specific, 151–154; human resources unit participation, 214; language, 149–150; team member, 148–149, 214; technology, 220
traveling, 220–221
trust: communication and, 90–91, 93; company example of, 95–96; cultural differences, 94; definition of, 82; geographic distance effects, 28, 34; guidelines for developing, 87–95; imperative need for, 86–87; importance of, 82–83; team member benefits of, 86; vision of team and, 79; work processes and, 95. *See also* swift trust

universalistic culture, 23

videoconferencing: advantages and disadvantages of, 127, 219; company example of, 106–107; description of, 122

virtual meetings, 131
virtual office, 128
virtual reality, 134
vision of team: challenges, 76–77; charter, 72–74; clarity of, 93–94; company examples of, 70, 75–76, 78–79; cultural diversity addressed in, 77; description of, 48; development of, 69–70; direction setting purpose of, 68; elements of, 68; function of, 67–69; globalness in, 69; guidelines for, 71–72; identity secondary to, 76; implementing of, 70–71; leader's role in creating, 48, 57, 69–70; mission statement, 74–75; need for, 67–69; purpose of, 71; tasks for achieving, 71; trust and, 79

Ward, Karen, 216
web sites, 229–232
whiteboards, 122, 126
Whitwam, David, 207
wide-area network, 134
workflow systems, 121
World Wide Web, 132